BARBARA ROSE, Ph.D.

KNOW YOURSELF

Also by Barbara Rose, Ph.D.

Stop Being the String Along:
A Relationship Guide to Being THE ONE

If God Was Like Man:
A Message from God to All of Humanity

Individual Power:
Reclaiming Your Core, Your Truth and Your life

If God Hears Me, I Want an Answer!

KNOW YOURSELF: A Woman's Guide to Wholeness, Radiance & Supreme Confidence

The Rose Group
Uplifting Humanity One Book at a Time
Florida, USA

ISBN: 0974145734
EAN: 978-0-9741457-3-0

You may contact the author through her website:
www.borntoinspire.com

Cover and interior design and layout by Words Plus Design,
www.wordsplusdesign.com

1. Self Help
2. Self-Actualization
3. Women's Studies
4. Motivation
5. Inspiration

Know Yourself is a true gift for any woman on a path of growth and awakening. Barbara Rose writes with the compassion, wisdom and vision that only a true transformational teacher can possess. Her love shines through on every page, and will open, heal and uplift your heart.

— Barbara De Angelis, Ph.D.
#1 NY Times bestselling author of 14 books including *How Did I Get Here? Finding Your Way to Renewed Hope & Happiness When Life and Love Take Unexpected Turns*

Know Yourself is an empowering resource for those seeking the truth about themselves. With the wisdom and grace of a wise and compassionate friend, Dr. Barbara Rose offers great insight and encouragement on the path to self-realization.

— Julia Rogers Hamrick
Author of *Recreating Eden*

In this profound book, Barbara will teach you how to get to know your authentic self. The guidance and insight in this book can save you years of self analysis and connect you with this powerful aspect of yourself who is always whole and complete, regardless of your life circumstances. A must read book for anyone who would like to live life more fully.

— Dr. Bob Gottfried
  Psychotherapist, Neuro-Cognitive Specialist,
  Author of *Shortcut to Spirituality: Mastering the Art of Inner Peace*

Know Yourself is a must read for any woman who is ready to remember who she really is at the Soul level and to discover her path to self-acceptance and empowerment. Barbara's words, once again, reach the deepest part of our Being by shining a light on truth, love, and compassion.

— Linda Salazar
  Creator and narrator of the audio program *Awaken the Genie Within: Manifesting Your Heart's Desire*

Beautifully written and divinely inspiring, *Know Yourself* is Barbara's best work yet! Barbara's depth of heartfelt compassion captures readers and opens their hearts and minds to the possibility of experiencing self-awareness to an unimaginable degree. Barbara is a truly unique and deeply inspiring person who has devoted herself to a life of service, helping others with her gifts of love, wisdom, and guidance. In this book, she gracefully leads the way toward self-knowledge by example. Do you dare to follow her on the path toward knowing yourself, your heart, your soul, and your divine purpose in this world?

— Ashleigh Stewart-Ghabi, B.MS.C.
  Author of *Understanding Your Chakras & the Essence of Colour*

Writing with personal wisdom and divine guidance, Dr. Barbara Rose touches the heart. Her work facilitates profound personal awakenings for those willing to journey into their soul essence.

— Judith Lukomski
  Co-author of *Crystal Therapy*

Dr. Barbara Rose's book, *Know Yourself,* is a spiritual map that explores women's life experiences from birth to the present day. It is a celebration of our femininity, creative expression, and inner beauty as well as a blueprint for discovering our true essence and purpose.

The beautiful look and feel of the book make it a perfect gift for yourself and all the women in your life. You'll definitely want to cozy up with it and spend some time nurturing yourself through its gift of self-exploration and discovery.

Dr. Barbara Rose is truly Spirit-filled, and her loving wisdom and guidance help you to realize the beauty that is you!

— Lisa Hepner
  Author of *Peaceful Earth* and *All I Needed to Know About Life, I Learned from a Rubberband*

With her wonderful wisdom and direction, Barbara Rose once again inspires us to reach our full potential. I urge you to read her new book, *Know Yourself,* where the path to positive change can be found.

— Carolyn Ann O'Riley
  Author of *The Path to Discovery,* Book IV of the collection *Archangel Michael Speaks*

BARBARA ROSE, Ph.D.

KNOW YOURSELF

A Woman's Guide to
Wholeness, Radiance
& Supreme Confidence

The Rose Group
Uplifting Humanity One Book at a Time

Contents

Chapter 6 – Adulthood: Wisdom on the Path to Wholeness 91

Chapter 7 Retraining Your Mind 105

Chapter 8 – Abuse: How to Spot It, What to Do about It, How to Get Out of It 119

Preface

How can you be in your body, live your life, and yet not know yourself?

I noticed this lack of knowledge in many women who consulted me from different countries around the world, and I discovered that nearly all of them did not know their life purpose. Neither did they know what they loved. They didn't have a sense of who they were. Do you?

Do you know your life purpose, or what you are here on this earth to do?

Do you know what you love or require in order to live your life passionately?

Do you know your preferences regarding sex? Do you know why you wanted a certain relationship?

I wrote this book for women because women today are taking an unprecedented leap in consciousness as well as with respect to their roles in society.

And yet many who are in a place of so-called status still do not truly know themselves.

This journey to know yourself must begin at the beginning of your life. As we travel this path together we will uncover who you really are, why you have not known yourself, and how you can reclaim that vibrant child you once were—before you forgot who you are.

This book is dedicated to you. To your divine feminine and masculine attributes, integrated into wholeness.

I share much of myself in the following pages, because we all can learn from the depths each of our sisters has reached, and rise by virtue of our painful lessons—together.

Now it is time to know yourself.

— Barbara Rose, Ph.D.

Chapter 1

Birth to Age Eight

From the moment you were born, you were whole and complete.

You had every attribute you carry today. You had every talent that you know about, and perhaps some that you are not yet aware of.

Your personality was within, awaiting expression as you grew and learned how to express yourself. Not a single part of you was "less than" any part of another human being, even if you were born with physical challenges. Each person has challenges—some are just more apparent to the eye than others.

You began your life with a cry. How often have you cried? Many times—just as I have.

Your tears and the sound of your cry let you know what you had: a voice. At birth you had enough power in your voice to bring smiles to everyone who heard your cry—because they knew it meant you were alive.

How differently we look at crying today.

This chapter will take you back to all you innately knew yourself to be as a baby—and have since forgotten.

You had caregivers. Some may have been nurturing and gentle, and some may have been harsh and judgmental.

During your early years, you learned from the adults around you which of your characteristics to display and which to cover up. From their responses, you learned how to behave. You took on their beliefs about what was good and bad, acceptable and unacceptable. In your adult life, you continue to block out what you learned as a child was unacceptable.

For many women, myself included, anger was unacceptable.

I was scolded or hit for expressing appropriate anger. As a result, for decades I stifled my anger, only to have it seep out in unconscious, destructive patterns, as I tiptoed my way around what I had learned was inappropriate—expressing myself.

What did you learn was inappropriate? Was it speaking out? Asking questions? Did you learn that you shouldn't rock the boat but should docilely go along with what the grown-ups were doing just because they said so?

Did you learn to cater to others to win approval and validation? Did you find that once you learned that pattern, it was like a vicious cycle? I did. No matter how much I gave and did, I still never felt validated. I still searched for approval.

I was searching for me, but I had long forgotten that bold me who lay dormant beneath the façade of docile behavior. I was in self-preservation mode, and I thought the only way to survive was to be approved, which meant behaving their way, not mine. Did you ever feel you had to forsake your truth in order to win approval?

Between birth and age eight, we were cheered for certain traits, and as adults we allow those traits full expression in our lives. We were also jeered for certain traits, and it can take years of therapy to bring out those traits again—healing us back to the wholeness we had on the day we were born.

What traits do you view as wrong or bad? I would venture to say that those traits were viewed in a negative light by the adults in your life while you were young.

I would also venture to say that if you had the courage to display those very same traits now, you would feel much freer and more alive because you would know yourself and your natural heritage as a divine, whole, and complete human being.

I ask you now to simply make a list of qualities that you view as wrong or unacceptable in yourself. This will bring to light how much of a damper you may have been putting on yourself without even realizing it.

When that list is complete, write down the traits and characteristics of the women you look up to and admire most.

Do they have a voice? Do they speak out with honesty, courage, inner strength, and diplomacy while they rock the boat? Are they sexually uninhibited and passionate in their intimate life? Do they stand up for themselves and show a backbone, or are they spineless wimps?

These lists are a vital part of this book. Please, now, on the following pages in this book, write down those traits you view as unacceptable in yourself; and after that, write down the traits you admire most in other women.

Traits I view as unacceptable in myself:

_____

_____

_____

_____

_____

_____

_____

_____

_____

_____

_____

_____

_____

_____

Traits I admire most in other women:

WOMEN WHO SAY WHAT THEY WANT
EFFECTIVELY

INTEGRITY

Do you see a correlation between the traits you had learned to stifle within yourself and the traits you admire most in others? Aha! Personally, I always admired women who were independent; who never needed approval; and who had supreme, genuine, glowing confidence.

Two decades ago, which trait did I think was unacceptable? Self-sufficiency. In my early twenties I falsely believed that women should get married, have children, and stay at home. While growing up, I heard that "a woman's place is in the kitchen, period," and I bought into that belief. That was what I had been taught. But deep down beneath what I learned to do in order to gain acceptance and approval, after I became Mrs. So-and-so, I envied and admired women who were natural leaders. Women who were genuinely making a positive difference in our world, even while they were raising children. I was taught to validate my self-worth from the outside in: from the labels I wore, who I associated with, and the things I "should" acquire on the outside to gain approval and status in society. I was never *taught* to validate myself from the inside out.

Think of the women you admire, women who are doing certain things with their lives. Who are they? What are they dong? Now, on the following pages, please write down the women you have admired, the special qualities you admired most about them, and what they are or were doing with their lives. This is an extremely important part of this journey to help you uncover your true self, which will greatly help you come into wholeness.

The Women I Admire Most, Their Qualities, and What They Are or Were Doing with Their Life

AT ONE
TIME

_____

KRIRKE LEADER, FAIR, HONEST
WALKED THE TALK
(NOW I'm not sure)

_____

SUZAN - INTEGRITY, ABLE TO
HELP ME KNOW MYSELF, TRUST
MYSELF

_____

MOTHER - COMPASSION & CARING

GRANDMOTHER PALMER - joked
and said what she wanted

_____

JUANITA - A supporter & protector

CARMALITA - a good leader

_____

_____

_____

_____

Can you see that you do have those qualities, the ones you admire, within you right now? Oh yes, you do! If you didn't have parallel qualities within you, you wouldn't admire them in other women. Those qualities within you serve as mirrors; they encourage you to see your wholeness.

To Know Yourself Is to Own Yourself

The traits that you have learned to disown within yourself are the very traits that will set you free to be all of who you truly are—once you own them.

How can you own the traits you have disowned? Think of every area in your life that is not as you would prefer it to be. Those are the precise areas in which you have disowned certain traits within yourself. Your discouragement, frustration, and turmoil in those areas is trying to show you that you need to own the traits you have within in order to live a fulfilled life. This growth, this owning must begin within you.

I will give you an example from my life that I touched on earlier.

In my personal relationships, I gave my power away. I was afraid to speak up in the moment and clearly state what I was unhappy about. I was afraid of loss. I was afraid of losing love. So I gave up much of myself until I finally learned to own that part within while I simultaneously learned I was safe and would not lose my own self-love if I spoke up. I learned I could speak up graciously. I learned that I did not have to sacrifice my truth in order to be true to another.

This process took many years and many painful relationships, until the tears brought a recognition within myself. The recognition was that to receive the love I deserved from others, I first had to learn to love myself. I had to learn to honor myself and not give that away because of my fear of loss. I had to learn that the fragmented part of myself that I disowned in childhood (speaking up) had to be reclaimed in order for me to heal myself back into wholeness.

It is usually during our earliest years that we split from wholeness.

It is those aspects of ourselves that we disowned and split from our wholeness that we must fully integrate again. Only in that way will you become whole and truly know yourself.

What Were You Told to Disown Within Yourself?

During your childhood, either through direct words, indirect actions, actual punishment and abuse, or subtle digs into your little being, you were told to disown a certain part of you.

What were the negative messages you were given? What names were you called? What were the most common insults and demeaning remarks people said to you? This is your chance to uproot them and bring them into your conscious awareness. Now you will actually be able to look at the list and see the negative messages you have bought into. Please write them down on the following pages. It is so important that you do this. The old, negative views you still believe about yourself must be uprooted before the truth can be planted in their place to consciously bring you back into wholeness.

Negative Messages I Was Given
About Me

A YOU ASK TOO MANY QUESTIONS

SUNSHINE (hated nickname used seriously by my brother)

Questions were ignored (you didn't need to know)

DISMISSED my OPINIONS as NOT important

MY CONCERNS were not important

B TOO QUIET

TOO SKINNY

B TOO INTO SELF (PLAY w/ OTHERS!)

TOO SELFISH, greedy

TOO BABYISH

TOO QUICK TO JUDGE

A TOO SMART FOR OWN GOOD

A TOO DEMANDING

A TOO PICKY

Now, to help you with your personal growth and transformation, I am guiding you to disprove each negative message. I want you to show yourself how false those messages were. They were not a part of you when you were born. They were a part of the dysfunctional and false comments from others that you took on. Here is an example from my own life to help you with this process. Two of the negative names I was called from age six were "dumb" and "stupid." I believed that lie until I was well into my thirties. To disprove that false message, I took stock of my observable actions, actions in which I displayed intelligence, insight, common sense, and ingenuity.

Now look at each negative message you wrote down on the previous page, and on the following pages, disprove each negative message by writing examples from observable actions in your life that counteract the negative messages. Write down whatever comes into your mind, whatever observable actions are the exact opposite of the negative messages you believed. This will greatly help you to distinguish truth from fallacy. It will greatly help you to see how whole and complete you really are within.

False Message I Was Given:

TOO SMART, TOO MANY Questions

TOO DEMANDING, TOO PICKY

Here is the Real Truth about Me:

I AM INTELLIGENT, THIS IS GOOD.
I LIKE TO LEARN, I expect a lot from myself and others. Good!

False Message I Was Given:

TOO QUIET, TOO INTO SELF

Here is the Real Truth about Me:

Yes, but it serves me well.

False Message I Was Given:

TOO skinny

Here is the Real Truth about Me:

Yes, it was great, I want to be skinny again

False Message I Was Given:

SUNSHINE (too happy)

Here is the Real Truth about Me:

Not too happy now, but would like to be.

You can learn from this book and from many others. You can learn in therapy. But no matter how you learn, the ultimate test that shows when you have moved from disowning to fully owning all aspects of yourself comes in your actions.

Therefore I now ask you to write the three biggest, emotionally painful challenges you have faced repeatedly, and then write what you will do differently when you find yourself in those situations again. Here again I will give you an example from my own life to help you though this process. I was in a relationship that was verbally and emotionally abusive. My greatest emotional challenge was to face my truth, and admit to myself how I really preferred to be treated rather than continuing to allow abuse in my life. My victory in action was leaving the abusive relationship. Is it easy? No. Is it scary? Yes. You, just like me, must face your truth at all times and in every area of your life. It is only by living out your truth, when your mind, heart, words, and actions are all congruent, all perfectly aligned, that you will begin to feel whole. And as a result, your self-esteem is going to skyrocket. Once you live according to your truth on all levels, in every area of your life, *this* is what creates inner wholeness, radiance, and supreme confidence. If it did so for me, it can do so for you, too. Now, please write your emotional challenges and victories on the following pages.

Challenge 1 — My Greatest Emotional Challenge in Non-Action

_____

_____

_____

_____

_____

_____

_____

_____

_____

_____

_____

_____

_____

My Victory in Action

_____

_____

_____

_____

_____

_____

_____

_____

_____

_____

_____

_____

_____

_____

Challenge 2 — My Greatest Emotional Challenge in Non-Action

_____

_____

_____

_____

_____

_____

_____

_____

_____

_____

_____

_____

_____

My Victory in Action

Challenge 3 — My Greatest Emotional Challenge in Non-Action

_____

_____

_____

_____

_____

_____

_____

_____

_____

_____

_____

_____

My Victory in Action

_____

_____

_____

_____

_____

_____

_____

_____

_____

_____

_____

_____

_____

It's Okay to Feel Afraid

When I moved into a new area of growth in which I was owning my truth for the first time in action (for example, in a personal relationship), I learned that the first time is the scariest.

It is perfectly natural, normal, and expected for you to feel fear when you are reclaiming those disowned parts of yourself in action for the first time.

As a matter of fact, if you didn't feel afraid, you would not be moving into new territory—you would be staying in the familiar comfort zone, which has brought you so much pain each time you disowned your truth.

I can only tell you that as you shake inside, and put into action that which you have been so afraid of doing before, you will feel a fantastic inner shift. You will feel vibrant and alive. You will feel renewed—because you will be reclaiming a part of you that you once knew long ago, a part that has been trying to become integrated back into the wholeness you deserve.

This work is paramount in getting to know yourself. You must own yourself, every part of your wondrous, divine being that you learned to disown. Only then can you meet the world, and yourself, coming from that place of pure love, authenticity, and glowing confidence in whichever area of your life you have been stuck—until now.

This whole process is being given to you from that omniscient, divine source that knows who you truly

are, and is now leading you back home—to fully embrace every part of you that you may have felt too afraid to embrace.

Leave Your Childhood in the Past, and Bring the Child Within into the Present

Your childhood existed long ago. You learned what to honor and what to deny. You were raised to believe what others around you believed, and you were taught to follow rather than to be.

It is now time for you to say goodbye with love to all of the negative messages you were given as a child, for they are false, and they no longer serve you to be all of who you really are.

It is time to remember that blame must also be left in the past. Please take full note that the people who contributed to your life during your childhood did the best job they were able to do at the time with the level of growth and knowledge they had then. If they had known better, they would have done a better job.

Many people have been wounded and have acted out their wounds, pressures, and feelings of inadequacy or futility on the little ones around them because they did not know a better way to deal with their circumstances or feelings.

It is now time to release all blame, hatred, and resentment, time to invite that whole, pure, and perfect child you once were back into your energy field now.

It is time for you to remember every glowing quality you had within you from birth to age eight, and allow that child within to know that you are more aware now. You can protect yourself. You can live and express yourself in any area of your life according to your grandest preferences, and you do not need anybody's permission to do so.

It is time for you to become whole.

Now, it is time for you to know yourself.

Chapter 2

The Preteen Years

We must now look at our preteen years—from ages nine through twelve—in order to understand fully who we are.

During those years, we learned to compare ourselves to others, and those comparisons might still be evident to this day.

Our preteen years were filled with innocence and mystery.

We were searching for our own identity when we began to look at our friends, even if only to see what they were doing.

We wondered what it would be like to have a boyfriend. Perhaps you experienced your first pang of liking a boy during this time—or perhaps you noticed that you were beginning to bloom physically while your psyche remained innocent.

You may have gone through betrayal on the physical level, and you may have had experiences that you were not ready for on the psychological level.

During this time, we most often pull the veil of knowing over our eyes. During this time, we typically know deep inside what feels true for us, and yet we might succumb to peer pressure or parental pressure to cover up our spiritual gifts because the grown-ups who surround us might not understand. Many times, we go along, even if it doesn't feel true for us inside. Sometimes adults force us to go along; we are given no choice and are too young to be able to do anything about it. At times, just to be accepted, we stifle or push down what we feel inside to be our truth. Other times, we might be punished if we disobey. Sometimes we feel as if we're living with and among other people to whom we truly cannot relate or share ourselves with. As we begin to look around us, we see and feel everything that we can either identify with or not.

My preteen years were confusing: I had a woman's body and a child's mind, with a feeling of being different somehow, different in a way that I could not define in words.

I looked around me and often felt I didn't belong.

I tried to belong because I wanted to fit in, and perhaps you tried to fit in, too.

Fit into what?

Social acceptance. Peer acceptance. Parental acceptance.

We were trying in myriad ways to gain acceptance from the outside because we did not fully know who we were from the inside.

We may have tried to get good grades in school, or to look a certain way. But no matter what we tried, that sense of belonging was based on something outside of us rather than on who we were within.

You and I had talents and gifts that might have been stifled or honored. But no matter how much we were applauded or scolded, our search for inner knowing was stunted during these years—because we could not identify with soul wisdom on the outside. And I am sure you will agree that we could rarely talk about it to those in our lives at that time.

How were we supposed to know ourselves during our preteen years? By our surroundings and how we felt in our environment. During those years of inner innocence, we only knew if we felt safe and honored, or unsafe and dishonored.

Our achievements may have been wonderful or paltry—but we were never taught to honor our own authentic power. We were taught to give it away. And we were taught to measure our worth by the grades we received, the way we looked, the ribbons we won, or

whether we obeyed our parents. Our worth was all conditional.

So we were conditioned to tiptoe around outer conditions to get a greater sense of who we were, and our golden moments were when we received outer approval or validation.

Our most treacherous moments occurred when we forsook our own identity or truth to gain acceptance from the outside. These betrayals remained within our cellular memories for quite a number of years.

We learned adaptation. But we never learned self-honor. We learned to listen to everyone other than ourselves.

We learned to obey what others said as opposed to what was true for us. We watched TV and saw values portrayed that were the opposite of our reality. We longed for what was on TV, where the children were honored. Were you honored? At times I was, and at times I wasn't. Like me, you learned to adapt to a constant sea of conditioned responses in order to feel safe, secure, accepted, and honored.

You may have been honored for certain behaviors that to this day you call your strengths. You may have been dishonored for other behaviors, and you may still be grappling with how to grow beyond whatever part of yourself you have disowned.

It is vital for you to remember that we incarnated into this life to be all we came here to be. You do have a purpose, and yet during your preteen years you might never have been honored for your true inner gifts. You may have learned to stifle your greatest talents and attributes in order to keep the adults in your life feeling secure with the limited wisdom they may have had about you. Many adults might have felt threatened by your special traits. Perhaps they didn't know how to relate to you. Years ago, many people believed that children were at their best when they were quiet. It was said that children should be seen but not heard. As a result, few of us were taught to speak out and rock the boat! Few of us were taught to prepare for a life in which self-sufficiency, creativity, spiritual gifts, independence, and self-expression would be honored.

We were told to believe in the Cinderella theory, and to validate our worth from the outside in—and that alone has taken decades of pain to overcome.

You may not have overcome it yet—but you are about to.

Were you praised for being the real you when you were a preteen? I would venture to say you were praised for listening, or obeying, and perhaps for a talent or two that your family liked to see.

If you belong to the vast majority of women who were raised to believe in everything other than the core of who they are, you most likely find it quite difficult to learn how to know yourself when you were mostly praised for obeying others.

This is the hallmark of forgetfulness among women. You forgot who you were while you were busy

looking for ways to gain acceptance from those around you. Your wise soul could not relate to those people and circumstances, and perhaps you had few if any people you could share your truest feelings with—so they, too, became lost.

How can you know yourself when you can't talk about your innermost feelings with the people around you?

How can you know yourself when you are held to a standard of acceptance based solely on your observed actions or performance? Did anyone ever ask you to honor the wisdom of your soul?

I doubt that they did—because they had also forgotten the wisdom of their own souls as they played out the roles taught to them based on the morals and beliefs of the society in which they were raised.

Many of us were not raised in a society that appreciated lightworkers. They are people (and you may be one of them) with spiritual gifts who openly share and express those gifts in order to help others awaken and evolve in our world. Many times their spiritual gifts are not openly received, and they are negatively labeled as "New Age fruitcakes." You may be a highly evolved soul stifled in a spiritual closet. You may have wisdom within you that is so vast. And at the same time you may have next to nobody with whom you can relate or share, nobody you can even learn from.

This book is in your hands because you want to reclaim your radiance. You want glowing confidence. Everything you want is everything you've already got on the inside. I take you on this journey through your life so you can see why you may not feel so radiant or whole or confident.

It is because the confidence you had when you were born was largely squelched during your younger years, and in your preteen years your inner radiance was based on whether you received approval from others.

How radiant do you expect to feel when you seek approval from others? The more approval you need, the more deeply you have buried your true self.

The more invalidated you feel, the more status you seek in society. The more you lack trust, the more you try to control the outcome of events in your life. By "trust," I mean going with the flow, knowing that your highest good is always taken care of with divine guidance from the angelic realm and God, or whatever you believe is the highest source of pure love and wisdom in the universe, the source that is always present to assist you unconditionally in every moment of your life.

I bet you weren't taught about that sort of trust when you were a preteen. I would venture to say you are not alone in this.

Today, unprecedented amounts of higher wisdom pour over the consciousness of humanity in every society across the globe. Women at the dawn of the twenty-first century are far different from those at the dawn of the twentieth. Can you imagine how vast a leap in consciousness the women of the twenty-second century will feel? It will be light years from where we are now, and we can only get to that point by opening our gateway to higher consciousness through understanding and becoming acquainted with the higher consciousness that exists within our very own selves.

Building Your Inner Knowing

During your preteen years, a part of you did know more than you gave yourself credit for. A part of you saw through people, saw truth, and saw the distinction between who you felt you were and who you felt you should be.

The problem is that when adults teach us directly or indirectly to follow their dictates instead of asking us how we feel about what we are being told to do, the result is a split in ourselves. This split is most common but not acceptable.

When you are split, your ego unconsciously takes over your personality and slowly pulls the veil over your truth.

Now it is time to undo this process, which continues well into the teen years, so you can honor who you really are instead of who you have been told you should be to gain approval.

Chapter 3

The Teen Years

S ometimes peer acceptance is gained at all costs.

Many times we strive for acceptance at the expense of the higher knowing in our heart, our truth, and what we genuinely believe is good for us. We sacrifice it all for the sake of acceptance.

You may notice that the turbulent emotional struggles of the teen years often prevail well into adulthood.

You may notice that you are still trying to gain approval and acceptance via social status, material gain, being associated with certain people, the amount of money you have, or how much you own.

On the other hand, you may be struggling just to survive. You may have locked the door to your highest knowing during your teen years, and you may still be trying to open the door to your true self in order to shine.

How Do You Shine?

How can you shine? The way to shine is to become aware of every single value, belief, circumstance, position, and person that does not contribute joy to your life.

It is time to embrace the knowing you had within as a teenager and to reclaim that inner knowing so that you can finally know yourself. It is time to reassess your life as if you were clearing out a closet filled with things that you have held on to even though you knew deep inside that you would never use them. The real you, trapped in your teenage self, is buried beneath such items.

For example, you may be keeping a relationship that is not fulfilling.

Or you may be staying in a job you believe you must keep to pay your bills.

Or your credit cards may be maxed out because you buy certain items just to be accepted by anyone you believe you need approval from.

The real you is trapped in this closet filled with old and dusty beliefs, habits, and attitudes from your teen years.

During my teen years, I didn't have a healthy romantic relationship. As I said earlier, I gave my power away because I took on the belief that I had to please in order to be loved.

Guess what? That same old view continued into my fourth decade of life.

I had to undo all of the old beliefs one by one in order to reclaim my own truth.

Once I did, I was free.

Once you make a list of every job, activity, relationship, and belief that is holding you back, you will see that the closet of your adult life is still filled with the belief garments you wore as a teen.

So now it's writing time. This will help you free yourself, help you learn what is not working so you can replace it with what you authentically prefer that will help you glow with wholeness, radiance, and supreme confidence.

Do you want that?

Okay, then. Now, on the following pages in this book, write down every single aspect of your life, every belief, every attitude that is bringing you down or that does not contribute joy to your life.

Here Is Every Belief, Circumstance, Attitude, and Situation that is Not Contributing Joy to My Life:

_____

_____

_____

_____

_____

_____

_____

_____

_____

_____

_____

_____

_____

Now that the closet is cleaned out, what do you genuinely want to replace everything with? This is your chance to create the life you have always wanted based on your own truth and higher knowing. You need to write a list of each belief, attitude, circumstance, and situation you would prefer to have in your life. As you begin the list, you may feel stuck. If you do, just ask yourself what really matters to you in your heart, such as getting a job or creating a business that is more aligned with what you would love to wake up to each day. Or to speak your truth concerning a certain relationship. Or going to a certain place you have always wanted to travel to, a place that your heart has always longed to experience. Write down the qualities that you would prefer to show, the ones that you may have been too afraid to show in the past. If you still have difficulty creating the list, go through a few magazines and note the qualities you see in pictures of other women. This will help you to own those qualities within yourself.

The choice of what to put on your list is all yours. No one on this earth can create your life. No one other than you knows exactly what you love, what brings you joy, and what fills your entire being with passion. What you are about to write is the real you that lays beneath shoulds, societal expectations, cultural attitudes, and what you have been taught that opposes what you feel is true for you. Now, it is time to bring the *real* you up to the surface on the following pages.

*Here are the beliefs, attitudes, circum-
stances, and situations I would prefer to
be, feel, and experience as my grandest
expression of myself in my life:*

_____

_____

_____

_____

_____

_____

_____

_____

_____

_____

_____

The Trick of the Ego

Two most important things for you to know are:

1. There is no thing you can gain on the outside that will make you more worthy, lovable, or accepted.

2. There is no condition in your life that you cannot overcome.

The ego's domain is your past; the ego's big agenda is fear.

Fear. I learned that the letters in that word stand for False Evidence Appearing Real. The ego will try to keep you stuck with doubts, old memories, and past conditions that do not correlate with the domain of your soul, which knows no boundaries.

You see, you are an unlimited being, and you are here on this earth to express the grandest version of yourself, the one that you came into this life to express. What you wish to create all begins in your mind.

It is also pivotal for you to understand that the goal of knowing yourself has nothing to do with material gain; the goal is to express that which brings you profound joy. That expression is the reason you came into this life to begin with.

The Competition Fallacy

In my first book, *Individual Power: Reclaiming Your Core, Your Truth, and Your Life,* I wrote that there is no such thing as competition. That too is the domain of the ego, and it is entirely self-limiting and self-defeating.

Can you be me? No.

Can I be you? No. And yet perhaps you want to write a book. Guess what: I will help you. Just send me an e-mail, and I will happily give you pointers.

Help from Others

When you are literally revamping your life to bring out the uncovered inner wisdom that had been stifled during your teen years, it is vital that you have role models and a support system that gives you encouragement, support, guidance, and help.

It is also vital that you do not discuss your process with anyone who will undermine your growth or efforts, the naysayers in your life who only criticize you. As I wrote in *Individual Power,* "Do not seek advice from those whose shoes you would not want to see yourself in."

We can have supportive friends from all over the world online, over the Internet.

If you need a friend, contact me! I am here to support you and help you to know yourself because I know how hard it was to undo all of my old views and own myself fully.

Once the process begins, it is fueled with joy and exhilaration.

Once you begin to clear out all of the clutter covering the shining gem of your self, you will glow with wholeness, radiance, and supreme confidence.

A Time to Go Within

I sat under a tree to contemplate the wisdom of a profound book, *The Dhammapada,* from which I soaked up the wisdom that Buddha brought to humanity.

I was trying to let go of pain. Yes, the pain in a relationship.

During my heartfelt request to release pain, I asked God exactly how to do this.

The words "Give compassion and understanding" came to me.

I felt a deep inner shift, and I finally realized that when I sought to please others, what I was actually trying to do was gain compassion and understanding for myself.

As divine wisdom poured into my mind, I learned that when you give compassion and understanding, you are no longer caught in the trap of trying to get them from others.

This is profoundly freeing!

I ask you to set aside time each day to breathe, and to give yourself unconditional love and compassion. Forgive yourself for everything you have been holding against yourself because you are now evolving into the highest expression of you that you came into this life to be and express. You have been learning and growing. If you have been hard on yourself, now it is time to embrace yourself with love and self-acceptance. Your past does not constitute your future. Only what you hold in your mind from this moment forward will create your future. Ask yourself what you would love to do with your life. What would fill your entire being with excitement? What would you do as an expression of self that would bring you so much joy that if it were your last day, you would pass over in bliss?

What would you do?

Now let's discover exactly how to know why you are here.

Chapter 4

Young Adulthood

D uring young adulthood, we live from the ego. Your ego tricked you as a young adult, just as mine tricked me.

Perhaps you are outwardly searching for your life purpose, or perhaps you are still trying to figure out why you are here in this life to begin with.

Many young adults are focused completely outward—to obtain a degree, open a business, get a job, perhaps even support a family.

Were you ever told to go within and focus on what you love? I was not told that as a young adult. Most of us weren't.

But this is a new era, and I am bringing you back into your young adult years so you can see, and learn from hindsight, that which your ego may still prevent you from seeing. I want you to see from the wisdom of insight.

You looked for outer gain of some form.

Are you still doing this? If you are, ask yourself these questions.

If you already had everything you ever wanted on the outside, how would you love to spend your time? Garden, decorate, shop, cook, speak, inspire, travel? What would you love to do?

Who are you on the inside? What qualities do you possess that bring you to life?

What is your favorite state of being?

Ah—being—it is a wonderful state to be in. Living in this moment, fully content to the point that you almost wish you could capture this moment and hold on to it forever.

What were you doing in these moments?

Have you ever been so in love with the process of what you were doing, so blissfully engaged in what you were bringing forth from within, that all time and space was suspended?

Those moments, those experiences are why you are here. They give you a glimpse of the diamond hidden beneath the demands that the ego places on you, demands to seek or become rather than to be and express.

Your young adult years may have been troubling while you were trying to figure it all out. And yet all you needed to do was listen to your voice, your opinion, your experiences to know what felt true for you and what felt out of sync.

Here's an example. If I were to invite you to come with me to the back kitchen of a restaurant and peel one hundred pounds of potatoes, would you be excited about that? No? Okay. It seems to be easy for you to know what you don't like.

Now, if I were to ask you to come with me on a trip to Macchu Picchu and see a sacred site, would you want to join me? Perhaps yes and perhaps no. It would depend on your preferences.

To discover why you chose to be on this planet at this particular time, you must uncover from within the depths of your being what causes you to feel fully alive. What causes you to be and feel so whole and complete? I would venture to say it is expressing some part of your essence that enables you to contribute to others.

That expression may occur when you are fully engaged with children or animals or adults or plant life, or when you are speaking to an audience, doing volunteer work that you are passionate about, going on trips to exotic places, studying or teaching, playing music, or artistically creating. Whatever it is—no matter what it is—this is your divine expression, the expression of your reason to be alive.

Once you uncover this hidden gem from within the layers of old fears, negative self-image, and negative self-talk, you will know why you are here. I can only help you reach yourself; I cannot go in and tell you why you are here. I can only ask you questions so that you will begin to question yourself in solitude. This may take practice. So I shall ask you! What truly means something to you in your heart?

What brings you to life? What causes you so much joy that you would do it for free for the rest of your life if you could? For me, it is writing and speaking, as well as giving private consultations. I would do those things forever because when I do, I feel so alive, so filled with energy, love, compassion, and radiance. I feel whole and complete. I feel this way because doing these things is my life purpose, and it took decades for me to discover. That is okay. We learn much during the discovery process.

What I am trying to do in this book is to help you claim your purpose now, so that you can release yourself from the bonds of needing to seek or acquire in order to feel that you are good enough. It is not good enough for you to be stuck in a miserable job. You did not come into this life to live in servitude. You came into this life to live and express yourself with passion.

Young adulthood consists of outer "shoulds" that cause worry; they may have even caused you to forget why you are here.

As a young adult you may be following a path set by your family or the expectations of society. Or you may be seeking the status or material gain you think you must have in order to feel complete.

Do you want to know what will help you transcend all pain, what will bring you a feeling of such inner peace that you would not believe it is the same you? Okay, I will tell you.

It is giving love and compassion to others, and to yourself. It stems from a place within where you learn that the most sacred acts you can ever do are those that will bring benefit to others and to all of life, purely from your heart, simply because it brings you joy to do so.

You have a purpose. It is called service. Service is not servitude. The service I am speaking of comes from within your heart. The joy you feel from authentically serving cannot ever be taken away from you because its expression is you!

Let's say that you love to cook. Note that cooking is just an example to help you uncover your authentic self. Substitute whatever you love to do in place of cooking.

Now, if you love to cook, the joy of running a business that caters lavish parties or caters food to people in need would probably bring you great pleasure. It would be a living joy for you to cook from your heart, and bring that heartfelt, delicious service to others.

The enjoyment both you and they experience from the food you so lovingly prepared is the gift you receive.

Service to others is a joy—there is no greater joy in life than to serve from your heart. And you do deserve to be well compensated for your services.

At times you can give to people who do not have. But people do want to give and receive. It is a joy to pay for a catered meal when the food is good. So please do not think it is unspiritual to ask for a fee that will compensate you for your time. There is a quote from the book *A Course in Miracles* that I would like to share with you: *"Never forget, then, that you set the value on what you receive and price it by what you give."* We live in an abundant universe, and you deserve abundance for the services you share from your heart in your life's work.

When you do what comes from your heart, no matter what that doing consists of, your soul radiates and then co-creates with others to expand your service and share with joy to make a positive difference.

Perhaps (still using the cooking and catering analogy) you can expand your love of service by forming a partnership with someone who loves to garden and create flower arrangements for theme-oriented table settings. You see, when you are so in tune with bringing out your divine self-expression through joyful service to others, that is the joy of life.

Then you naturally radiate an aura, a radiance that attracts other people to what you are doing so passionately and makes them want to become a part of what you are doing.

So you can work with others who love what they are doing—and you will all experience the loving joy of serving from your hearts. In every field of service, from entertainment to the arts, humanitarian causes, scientific and spiritual endeavors, there are people who collaborate with each other. Their life's work is their passion, and they love to work with others who are also genuinely passionate about what they are doing.

When you live from your heart, follow your truth, and are passionately absorbed in what you are doing, you will feel whole and complete.

This wholeness cannot be given to you. It can only come out from within you. And you will also naturally attract into your life other people who will collaborate with you. When this happens, it is an ever expanding expression of your life's purpose. As a result, your life will be lived with exhilaration and joy.

I hope you see this now.

Realizations from Adversities in Young Adulthood

Some young adults realize they do have special talents and then come into full bloom later in life.

Other young adults see or know their talents but are not taught how to honor and express them. So they seek validation in other ways and constantly compare now to another moment of time, either past or future; thus they never feel whole, radiant, confident, and complete.

The past will never return. The only reason we are revisiting young adulthood is so that you can see from hindsight why you have not felt as whole and complete as you deserve to feel.

Women are nurturers. Women have vast potential that lies dormant. You are one of those women. The obstacles, tragedies, adversities, or hardships you have faced came into your life because on a soul level, or on an unconscious level, you chose to have those experiences in order to transcend ego judgments, blame, justifications, avoidance, and denial of who you are, which has nothing to do with what others have done to you.

Anne Frank lived in a concentration camp, yet her spirit gave from the purity of love within her heart that nothing could extinguish.

No matter what has been done to you, now it is time for you to love and have compassion and understanding for that experience so that your ego will no longer keep you locked in a mental movie of your past, a movie that causes you to feel as victimized now as the actual events did then.

This, of course, applies if you felt wronged in some way by another.

Many people I have met are just like you and me: our greatest adversities in life became our greatest teachers once we decided to seek a higher perspective rather than remaining stuck, feeling victimized. Once we took personal responsibility to create new circumstances from our truth, we began to create a new life.

Thank the adversities you have experienced for teaching you that you *can* create positive, life-enhancing change. You can feel inner peace once you decide to free yourself from the grips of ego, and release all blame, by coming into this moment, now, when you can make positive choices for yourself that will naturally have a positive rippling effect on the lives of others. The adversities in our lives were not brought into our lives to test or crush us; they were brought into our lives to strengthen us.

Here, you have a choice: Remain stuck or lift yourself up. It is all your choice. You can go for counseling, therapy, and retreats. But it is a simple choice that will free you from the bondage of ego and blame and past suffering, as well as future seeking. That simple choice will let you feel whole, vibrant, confident, and full of the inner peace you deserve.

No one can give that to you but you.

The answer and the cure come from your heart.

Be the love you want to see in this world.

Give yourself and others the compassion and understanding you wish others would give to you.

Love yourself and all others as you wish they would love you in return.

Express yourself fully, just as you love to see others who are passionately alive express themselves.

Be the example by becoming so in love with you that you would not harbor a negative thought or reaction or ill motive any more than you would take poison into your system.

And yet, everything that is not of love and truth is poison to your system.

Within your mind you have the key that will unlock the door to the highest state of enlightenment, a state that masters from all faiths have attained. It is simply a rebirth.

It is a rebirth of you. Now I will take you on this process of the rebirth of self so that you can understand it more fully.

Chapter 5

Motherhood:

The Ultimate Gift of Life,
the Divine Gift of Your Creation

The motherhood I am going to speak of now pertains not only to giving birth to a child but to the divine gift of giving birth to anything your heart desires from within the depths of your being.

As a mother, I can tell you that the process of giving birth to my children was filled with the most astounding love and tears of joy.

Twice, I set the intention to give birth to a child, and nine months later, my intention manifested itself in the two most precious children I could ever ask this universe for.

Like you, I have had difficulties in my life. But having my children was a process I adored and lived passionately from the moment I was aware of conception through the actual birthing process and beyond.

Giving Birth as a Metaphor

I want to take you on a journey into yourself, a journey in which you can use the birthing process as a metaphor for the act of bringing forth from within the depths of your being the exhilarating knowledge of what you wish to manifest and how to go about it.

This indescribably joyful process is filled with a glowing radiance that comes from the knowledge of a divine purpose in your core, a purpose that you can "give birth to" no matter what it is.

I gave birth to my children. Now I give birth to my books, seminars, articles, and private consultations.

Each one is filled with exhilaration and joy. Each one has a purpose; each one has a rippling effect; and each one was set with an intention to reach you—so that whether we have met or not, my work will add something of benefit to your life.

This is the joy of the birthing process.

Motherhood and Purpose

Being a devoted mother is a joy-filled process that never ends. Each day, each phone call, visit, and experience, is new; at the same time, they all add enrichment to the children I have given birth to.

The commitment to my children stems from pure love. This same commitment now extends to all people that I can touch with my work, through my career.

The feelings are the same: joy and passion, unwavering dedication and unconditional love. I want you to feel this same joy and passion with your life's purpose.

You and I need unconditional love because we are not perfect. We are growing and evolving spiritual beings.

We are here for more than one purpose, and it is the process of achieving our purpose that makes for a life filled with joy.

Challenge

There are always challenges—especially during the birthing process.

There are new roads, new obligations, and new areas of self-expression that we are learning.

It is natural to make mistakes. It is a natural part of life to learn and grow as we become our highest selves.

Just as the birthing process is filled with labor pains, the act of embarking on our true life purpose is filled with fears of the ego that try to keep us stuck in the comfort zone of our past.

The key is to face our fears and insecurities, and to bring them to our conscious awareness with unconditional love for self, so that we can transform them.

Moreover, we must continue to contribute, to grow and nurture what means most to us in our lives.

Overcoming Challenges

Just as we are not alone while giving birth to a child, we are also not alone as we give birth to a whole new aspect of ourselves and bring it forth as our unique divine contribution.

We have help from our higher self (God) as well as the angelic realm. We have the help of other people who share a similar path and are happy to offer support. We never do it alone.

When I set an intention to create something I love and want to share with you, I ask for divine guidance and help, and I ask for the right people to cross my path so that we can create together for the highest good of all.

It is only the ego that perceives us as having to do it all on our own. None of us are ever alone. With every breath we take, we have the help of our higher self, God, or whatever name you give to your highest source of wisdom and guidance.

We learn from the wisdom of others who have attained goals similar to those we wish to attain. But it is not the attainment that brings pleasure. It is the creative process that is filled with joy. It is truly miraculous when you learn exactly how to connect to your higher self, God and co-create with excitement, as opposed to worrying and holding back due to fear. Your mind can serve only one master: love and truth or fear and uncertainty. You must be certain about how you feel, and once you both acknowledge and feel your truth, then you will have the support you need as you follow the next indicated step that you are guided to take according to the truth in your heart and soul. When you ask for divine guidance and direction from your heart, become still and pay attention to what comes into your mind. Listen to the sudden ideas that come into your mind. When those ideas bring you excitement, you will know that you are, in fact, being divinely guided.

Triumph of the Underdog

Most people love the underdog who triumphs. Countless people have been through tremendous obstacles, tremendous tragedy, and they refused to stay down.

They set the intention to triumph. And then they asked for help, pointers, guidance, and direction. They followed the core of their inner truth and refused to allow fear of the unknown to hold them back.

Just like you, some of them had dreams that they were not aware of until their life was filled with everything but what they truly wanted, and they were not living the way they genuinely wanted to.

The Era of Light

We live in a divine era of light, an era in which our thoughts and intentions become manifest much more quickly than they did years ago.

Time has speeded up. Our evolution has speeded up, and our souls have made themselves known, calling to give birth to and claim our divine heritage.

Just as a woman has labor pains while giving birth to a child, many people experience deep doubts and insecurities before they finally allow their truth to come out of the spiritual closet. I certainly did. It was a painful process, and the pain caused me to question myself and ask myself what I really wanted. My pain and discomfort forced me to shine the light on what felt true for me in my soul. I chose to follow the path that I am now on, and each day is filled with joy, love, self-expression, and sharing for the highest good of all. As I said earlier, I give birth to books and seminars, articles, and many other modalities to reach people just as I am reaching you now, and to help people as I hope I am helping you now.

It is my greatest joy. This process of motherhood is the same as if you were my child. I am here for you, and my dedication and commitment come from my heart, to reach you and make a true difference in your life. This is what brings me the most joy in my life's work. This is my passion.

Now I ask you to ask yourself this question: If you were to give birth to a purpose that could come only from within the core of your being, what would that purpose be? What would you want and love to do so much that you would be willing to step out of your comfort zone, go through the doubts and anxiety, and finally rid yourself of them completely—so you could shine and contribute from the inside out? I know I asked you this earlier, and I want you to be certain within yourself as to the meaning and the purpose you do have. What you feel passionate about matters. It is your individual expression of the divine within that cannot ever be duplicated. No one on earth has your identical purpose. Once you feel your purpose, you will feel your divine essence, and then you will feel pure radiance and inner peace.

The Divine Feminine and Masculine

Women are not only nurturers. We are achievers who have every divine quality that men have, just as men have nurturing. At this point of human evolution, men are just beginning to feel comfortable expressing their nurturing aspect.

It is vital for you to know that to be whole and complete, your most cherished feminine qualities must be as honored and expressed as your masculine attributes. This is what will bring you back into wholeness. Every fragmented part of your personality that does not honor a certain aspect of you is now calling out to you to be acknowledged and loved.

The most painful part of giving birth to your true self is to face the qualities you deem to be unworthy and to love yourself unconditionally for having them—because they are a part of you.

Every quality you have is divine. Knowing how to honor and display your qualities comes with patience, and love—to bring your highest self out from within.

Your New Life

The landscape of the life before you is filled only with your intentions, focus, motives, and actions to create what you wish to see manifest in your life.

Whatever it is that you would truly love to do, know that you can do it. Every single area of self-expression that you wish to bring forth from your divine self will be fully expressed once you decide it is time to do so. All it takes is a simple decision. Only you can make this decision, and once you do, you will soar.

Motherhood and creating new aspects of your life is a joy-filled process faced with challenges. The only way to overcome those challenges on every level is with pure unconditional understanding, compassion, dedication, commitment, and self love.

This is the gift you must give to yourself so that you feel whole and accepted by yourself, authentically empowered, and filled with joy to reach within and bring forth your divine self.

This is the joy of motherhood—and it continues for eternity. Your role as mother is never finished. But it is not a job; it is a joy. The thrill, the caring, the growth, and the dear way you touch the lives of others brings more joy than I can describe. It is unfathomable.

Releasing Self-Judgment

It is paramount that you release all self-judgment. The voice of the critical parent in your mind must be transformed into the voice of your dearest and best friend—and that friend must be you.

You cannot be effective, take risks, and expose your authentic purpose when you have much self-doubt and criticism blocking the divine flow of your energy.

You can only create and give birth to your greatest self when you accept all of yourself from this moment—now—exactly as you are.

The Manifestation Process

You set an intention to bring out and express your essence. How to manifest is quite simple, but the logical mind will be convinced only when you prove it to your ego a few times. Then it will be so much easier for you to manifest all you ask to bring about, easier for your highest contribution to reach the people who are looking for exactly what you have to offer.

Your Essence and Role in Manifestation

I am sure you have heard the saying "What you focus on is what you attract into your life."

During this point it is critical for your well-being and peace of mind to know that no outward manifestation will ever make you more whole and complete than you are at this moment.

If you have a desire to better any aspect of your life or to manifest more ease into your life, either for yourself or your loved ones, this is a virtue that you can carry with you and manifest for eternity.

The passion and determination you feel within your heart and soul are the forces of manifestation.

So as you wish to create or give birth to a new area of self-expression and manifestation in your life, trust that you will be divinely guided from within to fulfill what you wish to express and manifest. Release all attachment to outcomes. Attachment to outcomes causes anxiety. I want you to learn how to feel and be in love with the *process* of your life rather than the moment of completion. Now I am going to share with you seven steps that I learned many years ago, to help you with manifesting what you came into this life to live.

1. Decide. You must first decide exactly what you wish to express and manifest.

2. Be Willing. You must be willing to do whatever it takes, with dignity and pure motives.

3. Commit. You must commit fully to the process.

4. Let Go. This means to let go of doubts, worry, and fear about how it is all going to turn out.

5. Follow. Follow your gut instincts. Follow that still small voice within. Follow your truth at all times. Follow through with what you need to take care of. Follow the next indicated step. This is the process, and it is meant to be filled with joy.

6. Wait. Have patience. There are higher reasons why something is not happening right now, this minute. Perhaps two weeks or two months from now will turn out to be a better time to manifest what you

are working to bring about. Trust that delays are *always* beneficial. It will all turn out according to what is for your highest good.

7. Have. One day you will look back and see that you actually have in your life the full essence of what you first decided to manifest.

Desire and Outcomes

No matter what you have or don't have, no matter how much you have accumulated or how much you achieve, you will never feel whole and complete until you look at yourself in the mirror and feel your wholeness and completeness as you are now.

All manifestation and desire must be a true expression of self: to be of service, to contribute, and to make a difference—the difference you came into this life to create.

If you set conditions on your self-worth—conditions such as marrying a certain person or having a certain home or weighing a certain amount—you will be forever caught in seeking to obtain your worth. This process has put many people in a living hell of invalidation.

Did you ever notice women who have so much and still feel insecure? I used to be one of them. I used to falsely believe that outer stature would make me "somebody." But as I grew, I learned that we are all somebody.

A king is as much a somebody as a street cleaner.

The belief that outer stature makes one person more worthy than another is a fallacy. We are all equally worthy; we are all part of humanity.

We share the essence of our spiritual nature that transcends the ego's need to conquer and own. When you abandon that need, when you believe that you are in fact good enough as you are, you can claim your wholeness.

If you wish to express yourself in your highest form in this life, then you will find sheer joy and exhilaration during each moment of the process of your expression.

So as you look to make some part of your life more desirable than it is now, please do remember that this part ultimately must carry self-expression—one aspect of your gift to this world.

Your Role in Birthing the Life before You

Your role is to be filled with joy and to replace the belief that something will make you better than you are now.

This is the ego's trick: the ego will lead you to believe that anything will make you better.

Your soul came into this life to express your highest and best. It is often during the most painful and difficult times that you will discover more about yourself, what truly matters to you, and how you can make a difference for yourself and others after you have grown through a difficult period.

Being Radiant

Being radiant is being centered in your divine nature and truth at all times.

It is viewing yourself as a spiritual gift and as the creator of your life's circumstances instead of viewing yourself as a victim of your life's circumstances.

How you view yourself is one of the most important facets of feeling radiant. If you view yourself as "less than" any other being, then this false view will cause you to feel "less than." And you will suffer. On the other hand, if you view yourself as an equal and divine member of the human race, you will feel your equality and your divinity.

First you must incorporate right mindfulness; you must live as a conscious being. To extinguish any negative self-view is critical if you are to know peace in being who you are, no matter what your external conditions.

Many women have been through and triumphed over much. We admire them, their courage, their belief in self. What does it take to have belief in self?

It takes both living in your truth and having the courage to express your truth every moment of your life. Your truth is not negotiable. Once you negate your truth to please another, your self-confidence will greatly diminish. Alternatively, when you decide to be true to yourself at all times and under all circumstances, you will radiate with glowing self-esteem.

Belief in self also means taking a simple inventory of your true purpose, how you serve, and which ways of service bring you the most joy. If you are a parent, providing love and support to your children is a gift of service that will fill your heart with joy.

If you are a writer, the words you write might bring solace and understanding to others who are struggling, and so writing is an expression of a sacred part of your being. When you receive letters about the words you've expressed and the difference you have made for others, the joy is pure; but it is not a condition of your worth.

Whether someone likes the words you write or not makes no difference in your intrinsic value as a spiritual human being.

Spirituality in Your Creative Process

Your soul, your spirit is filled with eons of experiences accumulated from lifetime to lifetime.

During this new era, we are clearing karmic patterns, releasing all of the negative untruths about ourselves, in order to shine as the spiritual beings we are.

This is a time of deep cleansing, renewal, and new life. It is a sacred time in which every belief you have ever had will be called into question by the experiences in your daily life.

You will be forced to decide what truly matters to you, and how you wish to spend the rest of your life. If you are thrilled to be alive, if you feel that you matter regardless of what you have on the outside, if you are living in the moment when every divine and extraordinary idea is given to you—in the moment—then your life will be filled with much more peace.

If you are seeking outside of yourself for validation or to acquire something in order to feel you matter, this struggle will leave you feeling like a bottomless pit that can never be filled.

Your worth is never contingent on external conditions. It is contingent solely on inner peace and living according to your highest truths in the moment—this moment.

The Courage to Change

Many women face situations in which they are miserable, and they falsely believe they should stay in their miserable circumstances. This false belief breeds more insecurity and lowers your self-worth. To truly glow and shine from the inside out, you might just have to take some of the biggest risks that you have been so afraid to take, so the truth of your actions can match the truth you feel deep inside.

Once you take a risk and actually listen to your inner voice—the one that is telling you to rid yourself of any condition, person, or circumstance that is causing misery in your life—once you take the risk to be true to yourself, you will begin to glow and radiate more confidence than you have ever felt before.

You see, becoming whole requires complete self-truth.

Honoring your self-truth turns into radiance.

Living according to your truth and intrinsic joy of being of genuine service to yourself and others in your own unique way leads to both supreme confidence and a life filled with peace.

Nothing on the outside can turn your world upside down once you find your inner truth and live according to it in each moment and circumstance that you face.

No experience in your life can cause you to contemplate taking your own life when you are actually aware that experiences are just that—experiences—and they do not ever constitute your worth as a spiritual being, as a woman, as an equal member of the human race.

No matter what anybody has ever told you about yourself, if it feels degrading in any way, it is a lie—because you were not born with it.

Even if you have made many mistakes or have done many things "wrong" in your life, your soul is still pure and you can follow your truth. Thus you can create an entire new life from the bottom up once you realize that the supreme moment of now is your starting point—as well as the place you must always stay if you are to be focused, effective, helpful to yourself and others, and the grand soul you came into this life to be.

The Process Unfolds

As you begin to honor your truth and face what this universe and your feelings are showing you, it can become easier to accept where you are now and to set the intention of how you would like to be of service in this life.

Always say yes to what the universe is showing you, rather than fighting it. If a circumstance comes into your life that you do not want, then ask for the higher perspective as to how you can transform both it and yourself, so that you are authentically empowered rather than emotionally crushed. Look within and ask yourself what you can do to come to the other side of any experience your personality does not like or that your mind views as tragic. There is light on the other side of our darkest moments. Look for the light, the higher reason, so that you can move in a positive direction rather than remaining in misery. When something you do not like happens to you, ask how this experience can serve as a positive catalyst for personal or collective growth and positive transformation.

The greatest joy in life is to be of service in your own unique way. Many times we discover our greatest area of service as a result of our greatest hardships. Moreover, we often find that we are not alone, that others have gone through similar experiences. Then, we create friendships and work together, expressing our gifts from our hearts for the greater good of all.

A life that used to feel meaningless transforms itself into a life filled with joy when you honor your gifts and work in harmony with others to help them honor their gifts.

The Joy of Now

Where is the joy in life?

It is here. It is now. And by living in the here and now instead of some place in the past or future, you will come to trust that "now" is the greatest gift you have.

It is in this moment of now that all creation and manifestation exists.

Speaking your truth in the now is divinely empowering.

Sharing your gifts in the now is rewarding beyond measure.

Serving humanity in the now is the greatest service—so long as the service stems from your heart, with pure motives and intentions.

Speaking, doing, breathing, creating, loving: these are all done now, in the moment, this moment.

Your feelings of confidence do not depend on some future time. They exist now. The key is to uncover all false statements you may say to yourself, statements that make you think certain conditions will make you a better person than you are now. Once you recognize a sinking feeling inside as a result of a negative statement you have made to yourself, simply bring it into your conscious awareness by acknowledging the statement; then replace it with a statement about yourself that is based on self-love and truth. Cease all negative self-talk, and start to look at the inner gifts you do possess this very moment. Not in the past or the future but right now.

Some blind people create astounding contributions, and live lives filled with joy. Some people who have eyesight never seem to focus on what exists before them in this moment. Instead, they look forward or backward, and they are usually miserable.

Whenever I placed an expectation on a certain outcome in my life, all of a sudden I was filled with anxiety. I was worried, and nervous. I was insecure. How could I be sure about an event in the future?

How can you feel inner peace and feel whole, radiant, and confident when your expectations are tied to a future outcome? You cannot, and neither can I!

Once I learned to bring myself to center and live in this moment according to my truth, joys, responsibilities, and preferences, I felt all anxiety vanish.

You can live in this moment, too. After all, it is the only moment you have.

The Path to Inner Peace

By going through much anguish in my life, I learned the art of compassion and understanding both for all others and myself.

Rather than judging or criticizing, I gave compassion and understanding. Rather than seeking in the future, I learned to breathe, and focus on now.

This has led to a life of much more inner peace because the power of living in this moment is supreme.

The joy of feeling in this moment and accepting what is around you, as well as which changes you would like to make in your life, can only be achieved with much love, understanding, compassion, and focus in this moment.

If you wish to better your life, then you must release all belief that by so doing you will be a better person.

The key is in knowing that you are a supreme being just as you are and that "bettering your life" is just a means of self-expression. It is your divine expression to live according to your grandest preferences— not because it will make you better but because you are serving as a result of discovering and expressing the best you have within you.

There is a big difference between seeking to serve from your heart and seeking to "become" from the outside in. The former stems from purity and truth, the latter from insecurity and fear.

If you want to live a life that is an expression of self, then your path to inner peace begins with full acceptance of yourself as you release all blame, judgment, and criticism of the divine being that you are.

There is not another soul in existence who can be you or who can express herself exactly as you can.

There is not another soul who has your life purpose.

Some people may be on a similar path, but no other person in this universe can be you.

As you begin to see the grand and wondrous being you are from within, you will come to feel a great measure of self-appreciation. The ego will lose its grip, self-criticism will vanish, and simply living according to your truth and highest preferences will give you joy as you serve from your heart.

Service has many forms, and you are here to discover how you can contribute according to your soul's grandest state of being—as your highest self.

It is important to be easy on yourself during the process of your transformation.

Many women have so much negativity within, so many negative views of self that have accumulated. As you begin to shed the old negative views, the ego begins to go into fear mode.

You may feel exposed or as if you are being "reborn." But you are not being reborn; you are reclaiming your true self from the moment you *were* born into this life.

This is what many view as being "saved." What you are doing is aligning your soul's truth with your intentions in this life from this moment forward and saving yourself from future pain and anguish as you release the ego's need to be anything other than who you are.

Begin to feel who you really are. Begin to view yourself as you would a child who was just born. You are that child!

You may have had many experiences during which you took on views of yourself based on fear or self-protection; and in the process, you blanketed your true self.

Consciously awakening to self-truth involves a deep process. It requires steady focus in the now. It requires that you shed all judgment and self-recrimination. It requires an open, compassionate, and loving heart—even for those who have committed many wrongs; had they known better, and had they learned how to achieve inner peace, they would certainly have done better on the outside.

I can only share with you how I have learned this process. I hope that by knowing how I did it, you can learn how to do it for yourself.

I have been through tremendous pain and turmoil, and now, no matter what situation I am facing—I do face it—and I choose to create the best that I can from it.

I honor my abilities to create in divine co-creation, knowing full well I am not alone. And neither are you!

We are never alone. We have the help of the highest realms of light in this universe. Once I learned to ask for help from the Divine, I experienced the miraculous results that come from asking, and I learned that we are all co-creators. We are all one. So if you wish to bring about a positive manifestation in any area of your life, remember that you can ask for help from the Divine. And you will receive it.

Radiance and Wholeness in Everyday Life

You undoubtedly picked up this book because on some level you have an inner void that you have been trying to fill or you feel dissatisfaction with some part of your life.

The next chapter relates most to adulthood and the wisdom many are trying to achieve in order to alleviate pain and suffering on every level of their lives.

Turn the page, and the answers will be there for you.

Chapter 6

Adulthood:

Wisdom on the Path to Wholeness

M any times after I thought I had "got it," I found myself responding to new situations in old ways that I thought I had outgrown. If that happens to you from time to time, you may want to refer back to this chapter.

First and foremost, wisdom and wholeness or true and lasting joy can occur in one place only, and that is within your mind.

No person can bring you peace of mind. No outer situation can alleviate a broken heart, worry, doubt, fear, or inner turmoil.

Any situation may bring temporary perceived relief, but the purpose of this book is to help you find permanent realizations and growth. Therefore, some of the concepts may seem different. I have found them, however, to be the permanent cure to all personal suffering in my life, so I am deeply happy to be able to pass them on to you.

The Negative State of Self-Cherishing

"Self-cherishing" is a term I learned by studying many books based on the teachings of Buddha, an ordinary man who attained pure enlightenment and tried to pass on to others the way in which he achieved it.

Self-cherishing is not self-love or self-value. Self-cherishing occurs when we place our ego needs above all else; when we are grasping, seeking, getting upset because someone may have said something our ego did not like, and reaching for sensory pleasure to temporarily fill a void within.

This is the ego trap that keeps us bound to an endless cycle of seeking.

Self-cherishing is what puts "me" above "you." This is the cause of most discord between people and nations. It even affects our planetary survival.

Because of self-cherishing, we may cut down thousands of acres of trees to build another shopping mall.

We may lash out at someone who is suffering, someone who may act unkindly toward us because of his or her own pain. Rather than extending loving compassion and taking into consideration that when people lash out it is usually a sign that they are in pain, we "cherish" ourselves and lash out in return.

This creates unnecessary discord.

The flip side of self-cherishing, I have learned, is cherishing others. There is a saying that self-cherishing is the cause of all unhappiness. When someone cherishes you and is kind to you, this creates harmony. But when someone is taking, grasping, unforgiving, angry, rude, hostile, or resentful—this is the hallmark of self-cherishing. It will lead only to pain.

"Equalizing self with others" is another term I have learned that has made an enormous difference in my life. To place all sentient beings on an equal field with me creates harmony. When we consider all of humanity as equal instead of placing any person or group on a pedestal, much suffering is alleviated.

The root of self-cherishing is known as desirous attachment.

When we are attached to something, we are either anxious about receiving it or anxious about losing it. Either way, we feel anxiety.

When we feel desirous attachment, we are under the illusion that we *own* a person, place, or thing, an illusion that it is *ours*; this fallacy is created by our own egos in an effort to find some measure of security from outside ourselves instead of from within.

When we pass on after this life, all we have ever owned is no longer ours. This includes people. We can share our lives with people we love and care about; however, having a sense of ownership and being overly attached always causes pain.

Freeing the Mind of Pain

You are certainly free to enjoy anything that comes and goes in life, but to hold on for dear life often causes such a high level of stress that it may even take your life. You can free your mind of pain and free yourself from experiencing agony in only one way: shed light on all you are attached to, and release the attachment.

Releasing desirous attachment comes with seeing the true impermanence of all conditions of our life. Nothing is permanent, ever. You may have noticed that after a while, things you own no longer bring you pleasure. The feeling of joy and exhilaration soon fades, and you are left seeking something else to gain excitement from.

This cycle of desirous attachment causes much of human suffering. If each person truly felt fulfilled from within, then there would be no robbery, crime, stealing, or wars over land. There would be no political people who would do anything to hold the positions they are attached to because they perceive them as a way to feel better.

There would not be competition to beat the others in a chosen field. Instead, all would work in harmony with each other.

The illusion is created by the ego. You certainly didn't feel you needed anything other than love when you were a baby. You needed to be nurtured, loved, fed, clothed, and sheltered. Now that you are grown, a search for one thing will soon be replaced by a search for something else. Then, when your ego picks up a perceived threat that you may lose what you have, the turmoil comes.

The perceived threat could be a gorgeous woman, someone you think will take a man away from you.

Nobody belongs to you, just as you do not belong to anyone else. It is your choice whether to remain with someone or not, no matter who they are or what role they play in your life.

There comes a time when you must look within and ask yourself if all you have ever had, owned, or acquired in the past, including relationships, ever made you feel whole and complete and was the source of permanent radiance and inner glowing confidence.

This question will take you to the core of the illusion of desirous attachment, to the understanding of how so many people falsely believe that some thing or some person can be the source of permanent joy.

I have found that my connection to God and my having a pure mind free from longing and desirous attachment has caused me to feel supremely secure within. I know now that nothing on the outside can ever be a source of permanent peace of mind and inner joy.

I have learned through the teachings I have shared with you that whenever I was attached, I was in pain. To detach myself, I had to look carefully at the unhappiness I experienced whenever I was attached to a person.

Most people feel pain because of relationships. We all want to *be* loved. But—and this is important—all we can ever do is *give* love and compassion. Others may not know how to love us in return the way we would like them to, and there is nothing we can do about that.

This does not mean you should settle in a relationship that continuously brings you misery. This means you should remove your attachment to another person by understanding that he or she cannot be your lifeline to inner joy.

Cherishing others means that we view them as equal to ourselves. As I said earlier, this is also known as equalizing self with others. We can simply put ourselves in other people's shoes, with a sincere desire to understand their circumstances and how they feel, so that we can better understand how to relate to them and bring them loving comfort, instead of tugging at them to comfort us.

This requires a lot of inner peace and confidence. This requires a lot of inner security and purity of heart and mind.

Do you ever think that someone else can give you a happy mind, a pure mind free from anxiety?

This is also an illusion derived from the perspective of the ego.

The greatest way to release desirous attachment is to free your mind from the illusion that you will be happy once you have such-and-such or so-and-so.

All of the books written to help you "get" a man and all of the games you may have learned to play to "capture" the man you "want" are robbing you of your ability to release the need for the man.

The books may say, "Don't act needy. Act as if you don't care." Now how in the world are you supposed to be authentic and glow with confidence if you are playing a role?

The key message in *this* book is for you to glow by being your authentic self, releasing the need or desirous attachment, and freeing yourself from the trap of the ego, which leads you to believe erroneously that you must have something from outside yourself in order to feel fulfilled.

I hope you see the difference.

Women who do glow with genuine confidence, women who are whole, these women are in touch with their life's passion and understand how they can make this world a better place in their own unique ways.

Your passion does not have to be global or national in scope. You can love baking, open a bakery in your neighborhood, and feel thrilled by the delicious and beautiful breads and desserts you create for others to enjoy. As long as you truly love what you are doing and

are passionate about it, it is a natural expression of who you are. And you will then naturally radiate and glow with self-confidence.

Letting Go of Criticism

Another part of cherishing others is to, with loving compassion, let go of any criticisms made of you; blame the criticisms on illusions the people had at the time; for had they had healthy and pure minds, they would not have taken anything out on you. Instead of blaming them, cherish them for being your teachers— and for teaching you how to feel self-value despite anything they may have said or done.

Do not ever take to heart hurtful comments others make. Do not make them a part of your being. Know yourself and you will know truth.

Know who you are. What you believe in. What feels right and true for you.

If you dream of changing your career because of the passion you feel for a new field, enjoy the process; never let anyone stop you with their illusions of so-called failure or impossibilities.

Nothing is impossible.

I learned this saying: "Whether you believe you can or you believe you can't, you're right!"

If your heart is pulling you in a certain direction, then this is a part of your truth, and you must honor it.

This is where a solid sense of self comes from. It comes from knowing your truth. You can be sixty-five years old and decide you want to go back to school to become a doctor because you have always really wanted to help people. Go back to school!

Don't ever let chronological age hold you back. Many people, both men and women, have uplifted countless lives and have achieved their greatest self-actualization later in life.

Wisdom is the hallmark of a life lived from the heart, without judgment, and with compassion for all others.

No matter what it is you want to do, do it because it is a true expression of who you are. The joy you will experience by honoring what your heart and soul came into this life for will far outweigh the pain and disappointment you will feel if you don't honor your truth.

You are not here to be dictated to by others. And you are also not here to dictate to others.

True equalization of self with all others is paramount for a life to be lived in peace.

You may think you know better than others, and you may be correct. But you have no more right to tell others how they should live their lives than they have to tell you how to live yours.

This vastly important concept, equalizing self with others, will also help you to see the common thread we all share as humans.

Never put anyone above or below you.

Release all judgment of yourself and others.

Release all false beliefs that anything outside of you will bring you permanent peace of mind and joy.

Realize that expressing your joy in whatever capacity you can and giving from your heart whatever you are able to give are virtues that will reward you.

Avoid miserliness. I have seen people with tremendous greed; they either lost all they had or became fatally ill and did not live to enjoy all they collected while others in their families were barely surviving.

A great part of equalizing self with others and cherishing others is to put other people before material accumulation in your own life. You will never receive lasting joy from a material object, but a good deed done from your heart to help someone in need will always come back to you many times over.

This is important to remember because grasping is the hallmark of insecurity. Greed will only close your heart. How can you radiate wholeness and supreme confidence if you are so insecure that you live for "me, me, me, and my family only"?

You cannot. You cannot truly glow when you hold greed above giving and compassion, no matter how many justifications you may have.

It is fine to enjoy the best in life, but giving feels so much better than accumulating.

Remember always that desirous attachment is the trick of the ego and that when this brief life is over, all you have accumulated will no longer be yours.

Every good deed you have done from your heart will remain forever in the minds and hearts of those you helped.

Your heart will glow and expand by showing the true goodness of your nature.

Never "get back" at others; this will only cause you unnecessary pain.

Our times have accelerated karmic return. In other words, what goes around comes around a lot faster than it did decades ago.

Self-Rejuvenation

The core of self-rejuvenation exists within the center of your mind and within your thoughts.

Let's say you're miserable in a relationship. You can go to a place that offers rejuvenation, such as a spa, and leave feeling more physically comfortable; but your mind is still filled with anxiety over the relationship.

Self-rejuvenation requires examination of the thoughts that swirl around in your mind; thoughts that, because of the ego's grip on your imagination, build up to the point that you actually believe what your imagination is telling you. It may be a fantasy that causes you to feel temporary joy. This only leads to suffering. Just as you may wake up from a dream or a nightmare and see that everything is still the same as it was before you went to sleep, so too will your conscious awareness of the thoughts that swirl through

your mind cause you to finally see whether the scene you have created is serving your well-being.

Become the watcher of your mind and catch yourself when you have thoughts that lead to feelings of despair or exhilaration.

Focus on reality, and then allow your mind to direct your thoughts and actions in such a way that they serve the best interests of both yourself and others.

Regard what comes in and out of your mind without judgment, just as you might notice a small cloud floating across the sky. Any thoughts that first come up are exactly like floating clouds. You can choose to add weight and perspective to your thoughts either positively or negatively.

You can choose what your mind focuses on. You can direct your mind to love or to hate, to anguish and despair, or to positive life-renewing intention.

It is all within your mind. Every conceivable thing people do comes about as a result of what is in their minds. Some people completely rejuvenate their lives and turn them around for the greater good; others direct their minds onto self-destructive paths.

Now I will teach you how to become aware of what goes through your mind so that you can be more in control of your life and direct yourself to complete self-confidence.

Chapter 7

Retraining Your Mind

When you think a pleasant thought, you feel happy. When you think of a hurtful scenario, you feel pain.

Your feelings are the keys to help you catch yourself and take the driver's seat away from the ego, which only focuses on the past or future.

The ego is never in the now.

All you ever want to be is in the now—this place of massive creation.

Your choices are all made in the now.

So when you begin to feel miserable, no matter what you have or don't have on the outside, examine the storm clouds in your mind and notice how they have gathered so much momentum by unconsciously following the ego's direction that you find yourself feeling anxious, worried, and in deep pain.

To train your mind is simply a matter of becoming aware of exactly what is going through it, a matter of noticing it and acknowledging it just as you would a passing cloud, and then consciously redirecting your focus to something beneficial and positive.

This does not mean that you ignore or disregard a negative situation. It means that you turn the negative around to find the gifts within it and ask yourself what you can do now to improve your feelings and situation.

Some people hold on to misery for decades. Have you ever noticed relatives who have not spoken to so-and-so for the last thirty-five years because of some incident they are still angry about? Only a mind that is run by the ego could keep a person locked in the past that way.

A mind that equalizes self with others, learns loving compassion, and releases all judgments can be permanently free of the negative trap the ego loves to set.

Of course, you can understand this on an intellectual level. But say you are in love with someone, and they don't call you. Are you going to let your happiness hinge on whether your phone rings?

I used to, and boy, what misery I experienced!

I had to retrain my brain to focus on the now and on how I can bring joy to others through my life passions. This is what set me free from waiting for the phone to ring.

I rejuvenated my entire self through my mind and my perspective, while I sent others loving compassion and equalized myself with them; at the same time, I took people off high pedestals and honored them equally with all of humanity.

To feel important or respected, some people put their career success on a pedestal. This is all self-cherishing and desirous attachment.

What enhances life and brings joy is service. The next time you find yourself hinging your happiness on any external condition or person, ask yourself how you can instead serve from your heart, express, and create. Then you will free your mind from the anxiety that used to be your constant companion.

Practice in Rejuvenation

You may be hearing this for the first time or you may have learned it from other sources a thousand times: The key is to honor your truth, and really practice watching and directing your mind to the core of your truth, which takes great courage.

Any time I had a decision to make, I had to ask myself which course I believed was for my highest good and would simultaneously help me continue to be of service to others.

These decisions, these choices cannot be just about "me." What about you? If all I did was rejuvenate myself and never share my process, what good would that do? Not much at all. So rather than self-cherish, I cherish you. Any wisdom I gain or any experience I go through I see as a vehicle to reach you and many other people.

Say you are a teacher. You can have a profound impact on the lives of your students. Your words and actions carry far more weight with the little ones, and even with the older ones, than you may realize. In a way, we are all teachers.

Never discourage others or yourself from striving to bring out their or your highest and best.

Who Will You Love?

Now that I have shared with you how to retrain your mind and catch yourself when your ego has taken over, shared with you how to bring yourself back to center and direct your thoughts in a manner that will help you and others, who are you going to love and serve?

Ah—this is a great part of knowing yourself.

If it were just about you, then it would be self-cherishing.

It is about your divine service, your own special way to make this world a better place from your heart.

So many people have so much and do nothing from their hearts to help make this world a better place. Lack of money cannot be used as an excuse, either. Mother Teresa certainly did not have a vast amount of money, but she so dearly helped to bring a smile to so many people.

Now I'm no Mother Teresa, but deep in my heart I strive to be. So long as we all strive to cherish others and equalize self with others and treat others with loving compassion while we become aware of and release desirous attachment, then we are striving to bring out our best for this world.

We are then on the path few travel; but I hope many more will travel this path, because it is the one with the most joy!

I have lived like a queen and like a beggar. I have traveled most of the world and have had many days when I was hungry and without food to eat.

I have seen the best, the worst, and much in between. My wholeness, radiance, and supreme confidence did not come from outer achievements or from stature in society or from a man; it came from freeing my mind from desirous attachments and loving myself with compassion while learning to extend this same compassion to all sentient beings.

Sharing Your Process

If I had not had many books, teachers, and other people throughout my life who loved me, taught me, and even hurt me, I never would have learned how to release desirous attachment and replace it with loving compassion.

If you begin to feel a shift in your perspective, a greater awareness that can help you live a life with less pain and more joy, then I ask you to pass this on to others.

Share the concepts with others who may be in pain, and you will be making a greater difference than you may realize.

We all have teachers in our lives. It is important to find a positive support system that you can turn to when you feel confused or are going through a transition in your life or are uprooting an old pattern to replace it with a healthier one.

I have supportive friends who are always there to be of help and service, just as I am equally there for them, and for you. Yes, even self-help authors need people to turn to. If I hadn't been through so much and learned so much, how could I ever write about it to pass my lessons on to you?

Try to find a spiritual place, even online, where you can meet, call, or get together with people to help you on your path of becoming your highest self.

I am here for you, too, should you ever need someone to turn to. You can always contact me through my Web site and make a new friend.

I wish you the same peace of mind and realizations that I have found, those that have freed me from permanent pain and brought me lasting peace and joy. This is all I wish for you. Follow the steps. Go into your heart, know your truth, and then you will always know yourself.

Knowing yourself is knowing your deepest truth. It is the feeling you have way deep down inside, in your core self. That truth will never lead you astray.

Genuine, glowing confidence comes from honoring your deepest truth and knowing that you never need to explain yourself to anyone. You do not need another person's approval, permission, or validation. You need only your own. The key to real and lasting wholeness, radiance, and supreme confidence is to honor your truth.

It may be scary. You may have to rock the boat or take a risk or leave a miserable (yet all too comfortable) station in life; but once you do follow your deepest truth, you are on the road of no return. Once you follow what your heart and soul really feel, you will never, ever go backwards to dishonoring what you feel inside. It's always scary in the beginning. Leaving our comfort (read *miserable*) zone can feel like the scariest thing in the world. We worry about how it is all going to work out. We worry about what other people will think. At least I used to. Have you ever felt that way too?

I thought you would say yes. These feelings are part of every single human being. They are part of personal growth and evolution. It's scary sometimes! But despite your fears, no matter how your imagination plays out the scenario in your mind, just take stock of where you are at this moment, and face just this one moment. That is all you will ever have to do. As a mat-

ter of fact, that is all you ever can do. Our minds move into probable futures or memories of past events until we train our minds to face what is right in front of us and then follow our deepest truth in the moment. It's really one moment at a time. Whenever you feel afraid, remind yourself that all you have to deal with is this moment. Not next week, just right now.

Next, ask yourself how you really feel right now. What is your truth? What do you really prefer? Replace the word *should* with the word *prefer*. This alleviates all guilt, and places you in charge of your life.

You prefer to pay your electric bill so that you have electricity. You prefer to do only what feels entirely true and comfortable to you. Never back down from your real truth. Backing down leads only to misery and insecurity. Stop asking other people what they think, and get into the habit of asking yourself what you think.

I must share a story with you here. You may have heard it, but it's always a good reminder about following your truth.

Back in the 1970s, in the United States, a college student named Fred had to write a term paper in which he was to create a new business model. He wrote the paper using his own new ideas. The professor gave him a C on the paper, and told him that it was one of the worst business ideas he had ever heard of, that the idea would never succeed. Fred did not listen to his nay-saying professor. He followed his own truth and started the business we all know as Fed Ex.

That's one of my favorite stories to share because it shows how you can really never go wrong when you follow your truth. Sometimes we fail at certain things in life. We also learn so much from those experiences. Every person who has made a significant difference in this world has undergone some adversity.

Once you are in the habit of following what feels true and right to you, moment by moment, then you will notice your self-esteem and your life begin to soar, and it all comes from the inside out. Knowing this intellectually is one thing. Finding the courage to follow through on it is what builds a rock-solid foundation of inner confidence that nothing can shake.

Do you know how many times my relatives told me to "get a real job," as if being an author, public speaker, and spiritual teacher was not a real job. I just thanked them for their opinion and proceeded to do what felt true to me. I learned that as long as my motives are pure, and as long as what I want to do feels true and right, then it is true and right.

A Lesson about Delays

Delays are always beneficial. They are always a gift or a blessing in disguise. Sometimes we want what we want right now. But right now may not be the best time in terms of the overall picture. Maybe a month or year later will be a much better time. It could be that we might need to meet certain people to work with cooperatively. It could be that we are so attached to what we want that we get impatient. Whenever the

universe brings you a delay, remember that there is a higher reason for it, always for your highest and best interest; one day, in hindsight, you will see why or how the delay worked out for the best.

Hitting Brick Walls

Let's say you are determined to do something, but you keep hitting a brick wall, and it seems that things just won't fall into place. That means it is time to take a step back. It is a time that calls for trust. When you set out to do something and it does not fall into place, you can be certain this means it is not for your highest good, and it is best to let it go.

If you are trusting, and living in the moment, then take a few deep breaths and ask God, or whoever you believe in as the source of all-knowing wisdom, to give you a new idea, the highest perspective; then sleep on it. When you ask for a new realization just before going to sleep, you will usually find that you wake up with a fresher perspective, and much of the confusion will be gone. Ask for clarity. Ask for a new realization to come into your mind. Stop trying to figure it out all on your own.

You may not believe in spirituality, but whether you believe or not, it can only help you to ask for a higher perspective to come into your mind. I can promise you that you will receive it.

No Compromises on Your Gut Feelings

Your gut feelings are pure, divine wisdom. They go beyond what your five senses can ever show you, and they transcend what anyone can ever say to you. Your gut will never lie to you. No matter who says what to you, if you have a gut feeling, always follow it without question. If you feel unsure inside, it's a good idea to turn that feeling into a decision called no. I am not speaking about fear, such as fear of making life-enhancing choices and decisions. I am speaking about having a gut feeling in which something just doesn't feel right to you. This is what you have to follow. Never allow another person to talk you out of your gut feelings, ever.

Knowing Yourself and Trusting Yourself

Your fears may stem from not knowing how to trust yourself. You have to start by trusting your feelings. This is your truth. When you know how you feel, and you align yourself with those feelings, then you become your own best friend. This leads to tremendous wholeness, radiance, and supreme confidence. You know what you think and how you feel, and most importantly, you follow through with your actions.

When your thoughts, feelings, words, and actions are all aligned, they are congruent. This is wholeness rather than inner fragmentation, a fragmentation that is the foundation of insecurity, feeling split apart inside, and being overrun by fears and imaginary or perceived threats to your survival. It takes a lot of inner courage to follow through on your truth. It takes guts to feel, think, say, and do what is true for you, despite what others say, and even despite your own fears about how it's all going to turn out.

Everything will turn out fine when you follow your truth in the moment. No one can live your life for you, and I hope that you will only allow yourself to live the life that you really want to live. It all comes from within you as you bring it into expression one moment at a time. That is all it takes. Once you begin to live this way, the wholeness becomes more solid. Your radiance becomes glowing. Your level of inner confidence begins to soar—and it's not cocky ego but genuine confidence, which is also called certainty. You are certain about who you are, why you are here, what it is that you love, and what you truth or feelings are telling you moment by moment. If you live your life in this way, I can guarantee that you will come to find an inner peace and self-assurance with which you can weather whatever life brings. Moreover, you will begin to attract the best of the best into your life, because you will feel worthy of it. Once you have found your worth, based on your truth, you have truly come to know yourself.

Chapter 8

Abuse:

How to Spot It, What to Do about It,
How to Get Out of It

I decided to include this chapter about abuse because most women who feel "less than," most women who do not feel whole, radiant, or supremely confident are being abused.

Are you? I am going to describe the most common forms of abuse, and then I am going to ask you to write down how this may pertain to you. The writing will greatly help you see what may be blocking you from coming into wholeness. The abusive words and behaviors that come from another may be undermining you more than you realize. Perhaps they are not coming to you now, but they might have in the past. Perhaps

abuse is imposed on you every day, and you accept it because you believe this is just the way the imposer is; you keep the status quo out of a deep fear of being alone, without a partner, or without the material comfort or convenience you may receive from the imposer. But abuse in all forms erodes your self-worth and confidence. It is poison to radiance, toxic to wholeness, and lethal to supreme confidence.

Here are the signs of abuse. If they pertain to you, just know one thing: this is your opportunity to spot the signs and learn how to get out of the abuse.

Verbal, Mental, and Emotional Abuse

I am going to guide you step by step so you can see how all forms of abuse can only undermine the wholeness, radiance, and supreme confidence you really want to feel. It is my deepest hope that you not only embrace what I am about to tell you, but that you also find the courage to take personal responsibility for your well-being on all levels.

Verbal Abuse

Let's say you've put on a few pounds, or even 20 or 30, and your partner makes a snide remark: "Putting on some extra weight there, Hon; better get to the gym." I call that remark verbal abuse. It does not feel good. It feels demeaning. When a remark feels demeaning, it is demeaning. And this is verbal abuse.

Do not make excuses for observations. The one you love can "observe" that you are getting greyer, more wrinkled, less toned. The list could go on.

What matters is that you deserve to have someone in your life who loves and accepts you just as you are, weight, grey hair, wrinkles, and all.

Now, suppose you say, "Boy, I'm really gaining weight." And your partner answers, "Yep, but we all do sometimes. I love you for who you are, not the number on the scale." That is an unconditionally loving partner.

Do you see the difference? I could write an entire book about abuse, but I want to get straight to the point so you notice what abuse is.

Verbal abuse consists of comments that cause you to feel "less than." They cause you to have that sinking feeling in your stomach, that feeling of betrayal, hurt, depression, sadness, and grief.

When you notice that you are being abused—verbally or otherwise—you, my dear sister, have two choices: (1) you can keep allowing it to happen, which will cause you to feel even less than you have ever felt in the past; or (2) you can ask the abusive person to completely stop. If he or she does stop, this is fantastic. If he or she doesn't stop, then you are going to have to summon up all of your inner truth, all of your real feelings about the verbal abuse you receive each day, and walk out of this person's life.

If you have asked the abusive person to stop many times and nothing has changed, nothing will change. The abusive person will not stop just because you ask again. People who tell you to understand the abuser and to remain in the abusive situation seriously need to

reconsider their statements. I would never guide you to take abuse or to tolerate it, not even for a few minutes.

Verbal abuse comes in the form of snide remarks, put-downs, insults, degrading comments, forceful demands, controlling tones, and harsh words.

As a woman who wishes to feel whole and complete on the inside so that your inner glow shows on the outside, you must leave the abusive situation. There is no other way.

Mental Abuse

Mental abuse is a bit trickier than verbal abuse. Mental abuse is a pattern of behavior or speech that makes you feel you are being played with, controlled, and intimidated. When you are the victim of mental abuse, you find yourself feeling more and more insecure, less and less vibrant, and more confused; you feel as if you need to ask your partner for permission to do things, buy things, go places. You may even feel that you need to ask permission in regard to your spiritual preferences.

Mental abuse occurs when you are told what to do and when to do it, when you are ordered around as if you were in a prison camp. Mental abuse often comes disguised. For example, the abuser may conveniently have amnesia and twist facts to suit his preferences. Even though you know what you are talking about, the abuser tells you that you are wrong. Or the abuser may say he will do such-and-such, never do it, and then say he doesn't remember telling you he would do the thing to begin with.

To put it in a nutshell, mental abuse has you scratching your head and wondering if you are losing your mind. You wonder if it's you, if maybe you're making a lot of mistakes and hearing things incorrectly.

The truth is that when you feel this way, when you find that you consistently question your sanity, you are being mentally abused.

Control, manipulation, intimidation, convenient amnesia, harassment, threats, all of these are mental abuse. They threaten your peace of mind, your sanity. And one day you look at yourself and think you need psychotherapy. This is the effect of mental abuse. It causes insanity.

Emotional Abuse

Emotional abuse simply hurts. You feel extremely sad; you cry; you feel unloved, uncared for, taken for granted, neglected, and betrayed.

Emotional abuse hurts just as much and is just as deadly as any other form of abuse. It cannot be tolerated; there is no excuse for it; you cannot excuse it away.

I am going to share with you a couple of real-life situations. To protect client confidentiality, I will not reveal names or particulars. But the true stories will help you to understand my point.

I was giving a tele-seminar one evening based on my book *Stop Being the String Along: A Relationship Guide to Being THE ONE*. One participant asked, "Isn't it okay to take just a little abuse? I mean, no one is perfect." To which I replied, "I am going to answer your question with a question. If you put your hand in a pot of boiling water, take your hand out so that it can heal, and then put just one finger back into the boiling water, is that okay? I mean, it's just one finger—not the whole hand."

No! It is not okay to tolerate abuse at all, any more than it is okay to put one finger into a pot of boiling water. Abuse hurts!

Abuse cannot be tolerated at all. You cannot make or accept excuses because with excuses, you allow the abuse to continue. You must leave the situation entirely. There is no other way.

Here's the second real-life situation. I had a client who felt there was a wall between her husband and her. There was no passion in bed; it was like living with a roommate. He would say unkind (read *abusive*) comments to her, but she felt this was not all that bad. They did not have open, honest, and genuine communication. They were just going through the motions in their marriage, which was only a shell of what they had had years earlier. Through our private sessions, my client came into her truth. She began to honor her needs and acknowledge how she felt when her husband spoke to her in a demeaning manner. After a number of weeks had passed, she began to feel her genuine worth, dignity, and self-love rise to the surface. As a result, she was ready to leave the marriage. Then her husband did a complete about-face. They shared their feelings from their hearts, they consciously re-created their relationship, the abusive comments ceased permanently, and their marriage was re-ignited into a conscious union of two people who dearly loved each other and were equally committed to making their love flourish.

Here is the catch. For an abusive pattern to change, *you* have to change. You have to take personal responsibility to never allow yourself to be spoken down to. It is you who has to create healthy boundaries to protect your self-esteem, and at the first sign of abuse you must make it clear that you will not tolerate it. If the relationship is new, the first sign of abuse needs to be the last sign; you should make skid marks as you take off in the opposite direction.

If the abuse is a pattern in a long-term relationship, you must disengage yourself from having contact with the abusive person.

Guess what will happen? Once your self-esteem has increased and you create your new boundaries, you will naturally attract people into your life who would never dream of degrading you in any way.

Now, I created this book to help you go through your own personal transformation. Will it be easy? No. It will not be easy. Personal transformation is one of the most difficult, scariest experiences a person can face. It is an experience that will cause you to feel shaken up until the inner transformation is made.

What is required? Being completely honest with yourself. This is the vital key to personal transformation. Remember: if I could do it, so can you.

On the following pages I want you to write down the situations of verbal, mental, and emotional abuse that exist in your life right now.

If you do not have an abusive person in your life at all now, on any level, including at work or among your peers, then I want you to write down any abuse you have experienced in the past that caused you to feel "less than." You can put it all down—just as it flows into your mind. There is no way you can get this wrong. Writing this list is a crucial step in your understanding of abuse, in knowing how it has contributed to your feeling fragmented, insecure, and less than in your life. Write the list on the following pages—right here—right now. Please do this, no matter how hard it may be. It is for your good, and it can only help you come into true wholeness. Once you have made your list, I will guide you through the rest of the process.

Here is my list of verbal, mental, and emotional abuse: words, behaviors, actions, looks, gestures, contacts, and situations that hurt me.

_____

_____

_____

_____

_____

_____

_____

_____

_____

_____

_____

_____

_____

Physical Abuse

Now I want you to write down any time you have been hit, tied up, sodomized, sexually abused, molested, pushed, shoved, smacked—any and all of it. And include any time you were denied medical attention or treatment from abuse. Write down the incidents so you can see how you were violated.

If you cry, that is okay. I embrace you and honor you for your courage. I promise you from my heart that this will pay off for you.

My accounts of physical abuse:

_____

_____

_____

_____

_____

_____

_____

_____

_____

_____

_____

_____

_____

_____

_____

Recognizing Your Feelings and Setting Healthy Boundaries

Now, please read over your lists in their entirety, and allow your feelings to flow up to the surface. If you feel rage, you can hit a pillow on your bed. If you feel immense pain and hurt, please allow yourself to let it come out; allow yourself to cry. Feelings must be recognized; they must be allowed to flow up and out of your system safely. Please re-read your lists and return to this page when you are finished.

Okay, I know you are immersed in feelings now. You deserve to fully notice these feelings and declare to yourself that you will never allow abuse into your life again from any person—no matter who he or she is.

Now we are going to establish your inner truth and backbone—so you will actually feel a solid sense of self based on your truth.

From this moment on, whenever you notice any form of abusive behavior, I ask you to set a clear, definitive, and healthy boundary around yourself. Setting that boundary will allow you to move away from the source of abuse and to never allow abuse into your life again.

The Scariest Part

The scariest part of growth is like a dark cloud. Do you remember when I said that personal transformation is not easy? I said that because it is quite easy to read a book, listen to tapes, hear all kinds of wonderful people speak, and keep it all in your head but not integrate it into observable action. When I asked you to remove yourself completely from any person who is the source of any abuse, I bet you felt fear. This is natural. It does feel scary, and it is not easy to walk your talk. But you bought this book so that you could engage in personal transformation, not so that you could simply read paragraphs of airy-fairy affirmations and tidbits of useless inspiration.

When you feel something negative deep inside, this feeling is your dearest and best friend. This feeling is letting you know that such-and-such is not okay. Once you notice how you feel, it is up to you and you alone to become your own best friend and move away from whatever or whomever is causing you pain through verbal, mental, emotional, or physical abuse.

The fear is like a big dark cloud in the sky. It may look and feel terrifying; I know because I have been there too. But once you take your first step away from the source of abuse and into your truth, personal alchemy and authentic empowerment begin to take the place of fear. All of a sudden, as a result of your positive actions, you notice rays of sunlight peeking through the dark cloud. You realize that you will be okay; in fact, you will be better than you ever were before.

Now, on the next couple of pages, I want you to pretend that you are fearless. I want you to write down—as if you had no fear at all—what you would do to take personal responsibility to transform yourself and your life by moving completely away from any past or present abuse.

Please write this list. You are almost there!

I am fearless. This is what I would do if I weren't afraid to move myself out of misery and pain:

_____

_____

_____

_____

_____

_____

_____

_____

_____

_____

_____

Know Yourself

Now please re-read the list you just wrote.

Great! Now I want you to hold in your mind a picture of this new and empowered you.

This is the real you beneath the fear!

This is the you that your heart and soul have been calling out to for so long, via pain, to get you to notice so that you would transform yourself.

If you are feeling petrified of moving into your truth, it would be wise to seek professional therapy or spiritual counseling from someone who specializes in authentic empowerment and personal transformation as well as abuse.

It is not only good, it is vital to have a trusted support system when you are undergoing crucial personal transformation.

If you begin the process on your own but then feel stuck, having a support system to turn to only makes you a stronger person. If you feel you can take the last steps you wrote without any professional support whatsoever, then this is fine, too. Do it whichever way you can while bringing no harm to yourself or anyone else.

This is your lifetime, your time for creating personal transformation that is meaningful, true, and lasting.

This is your time to notice all you have put up with and dare yourself to become so much stronger, your time to watch yourself transform and reach the other side of the challenges facing you—because that, Dear One, is why they are there.

The challenges are in front of you so that you can summon your inner truth and courage, and moment by moment, either with or without professional help, face those challenges and overcome them at this time.

You wouldn't be reading this page at this time if it was not *the* time to begin the process you have spent eons trying to begin, the process of transforming and coming into wholeness.

Now the process is in front of you. You wrote down exactly what you would do if you had no fear. I can guarantee you that as you move through your actions into your full truth, you are going to feel and be transformed.

Please remember that all of us who undergo personal transformation cry and feel terrified inside as we face our truth. I certainly did. But if I could do it, you can do it, too.

You can follow the process by using this book and your lists as tools for personal growth, spiritual growth, and inner transformation. In the process, through self-love and truth and the strength to carry out your actions, you will see a remarkable difference in your life now and for the rest of your life.

You have your lists. I believe in you. If you need a friend, please contact me through my Web site, www.borntoinspire.com, and I will do all I can to get

back to you in support of your growth and personal transformation. You have a friend in me, and I honor you for coming into your truth and discovering the real strength you have beneath the fears, strength that will see you to the other side of this situation, as you transform yourself into wholeness, radiance, and supreme confidence.

Chapter 9

Answers

to the Ten Most Common Questions Women Ask Me

I n this chapter, you will find examples of the ten most common questions women ask me during personal consultations and tele-seminars or by e-mail through my Web site. There was a time when I asked myself many of these same questions. I imagine they will sound familiar to you, too. I hope my answers help you in your personal transformation.

1. *How can I know for sure if I'm making the right decision when it comes to choosing between my marriage and my mental health and self-esteem?*

I think you already know the answer to your question, but you may feel afraid of honoring your truth and taking a step in a life-enhancing direction because it feels scary to move out of your comfort zone.

You have two choices. One is to continue living with insanity and low self-esteem; the other is to stop sacrificing your self, your mental health, and your self-worth for another.

If you are being harmed by emotional or mental abuse, the only life-enhancing choice, the only choice that will allow you to feel whole, radiant, and supremely confident is to honor your real feelings, no matter how scary this might feel, and to move in the direction you know deep inside is for your highest good. The alternative is to live in misery. I hope that you find the courage to choose self-truth, and follow what you know in your heart is for your highest good so that you can come back into wholeness. The fear will pass once you take the initial steps. Then the fear will be behind you, and you will begin to shine.

2. *I want to know more about spirituality. It has affected my life deeply, and I want to have a deeper understanding of what it is all about. Are there any good places other than church to learn about this?*

Ironically, Unity Church can help you learn about spirituality. Unity Church is entirely spiritual. Without dogma, Unity embraces every person's religious and spiritual path, and teaches much about spirituality, manifestation, and how you are truly connected to God.

You can also go to spiritual conferences, where you can attend seminars given by authors of books about spirituality. There are all kinds of retreats, some held in one location and some that travel to sacred sites, that are wide in scope and offer many different spiritual paths to select from. I suggest following what feels right for you when you read about it. You can learn about many retreats online. Also, you can listen to live tele-seminars about spirituality (I give them all the time), ask questions, and receive personal answers.

And you can read books about the areas of spirituality that interest you, to gain greater understanding. Go with what you feel drawn to; on a soul level, this is moving you in the direction of greater spiritual growth.

Spirituality resides in only one place: in your heart. It's really not out there; it's all inside. As long as you follow the truth in your heart, you will be moving in the right direction. But the resources I've mentioned can always benefit you, as they still benefit me.

3. *It's said that you shouldn't fall in love with the potential of a person; that if you look hard enough, you can see the God in everyone; and that if you work on your own stuff, you can bring out the best in the other person and help him realize the God in himself. At this point, I don't know whether it's best if my partner and I separate or not. We have a four-year-old daughter,*

which makes it a more difficult decision. As soon as I decide to leave because the relationship is so deeply unsatisfying, he improves for a while. And I don't think it's okay to leave while there is a possibility. I have seen him in his full God-potential, which makes it even harder. But the improvement soon fades, and I get impatient with him and hard on myself for not being together enough to bring out the God in him. It's a self-perpetuating nightmare. I feel damned if I do and damned if I don't. It's exacerbated by the fact that if I left, he would be absolutely devastated. While I know I'm not responsible for him, I do feel we have a duty of care to others. Am I wanting him to be something he doesn't want to be, or isn't ready to be? Please help me with my confusion!

I went through much of what you are going through. If your partner is not taking personal responsibility to work on his own growth, to work on the relationship—not just by acting like a good boy for a few weeks but with a sincere desire to become the best partner he can be and as committed to the relationship as you are—then you are in love with potential, and it is a self-perpetuating nightmare! It hurts.

When you learn that your experiences are trying to get you to honor your real truth, you will move in the direction that is entirely life enhancing, set a positive example for your daughter, and attract a healthy partner who also honors his truth while honoring you and your daughter at the same time.

You can have a cordial and cooperative relationship with the father of your daughter, and share in parental responsibility with healthy communication for her sake. But at the same time you can get out of the chaos you have been living with, the chaos that makes you feel so deeply dissatisfied. Honor your feelings. What are they telling you?

If you have tried countless times to create positive change with your husband, and nothing is really changing, then please remember this: you can no more get strawberries from an apple tree than you can change another person.

He has to want to change and be as committed to the relationship as you are. If that is not happening despite all of your pleas, it most likely will not happen until *you* make a change.

I have heard first-hand accounts of people in similar situations who walked out of their relationships, got counseling, and whose former partners also went for counseling and did a complete about-face. They healed themselves, and they were reunited with the support of professional help, because they both took equal personal responsibility for their own growth. Then they were able to have a genuine relationship.

You must take the risk to honor your truth and follow through with actions before you can expect anything to change. Don't make a move as a tactic to manipulate the other person. Make a move that reflects what your heart and soul really prefer. Then and only then will your confusion pass. Clarity will replace turmoil, and higher self-esteem will replace the deeply dissatisfied feelings you have been living with.

4. *How do I relinquish my need to be in control? For example, my fifteen-year-old son has a girlfriend who will not talk to him about what is worrying her. It frustrates me that I cannot help him to understand her because I have no way of fully appreciating what is going on. I know this is ridiculous, but I worry anyway.*

Your need to feel in control is understandable because it arises out of a fear that the one you love may be hurt. Naturally, you want to protect him. To counter this fear, please understand that the best example you can set is to show your son that your own self-worth is solid, and to let him know that it is okay to learn for himself. It is even okay to make mistakes because mistakes help people learn. Letting go of your need to be in control requires that you give your son roots and wings. Let him know that you are always there for him if he ever wants to talk to you. Most teenage boys don't want to discuss intimate matters with their mothers. So you must respect his boundaries and his need for privacy as he learns, experiences relationships, and grows. If you criticize him or try to tell him what he "should" be doing, he will distance himself from you. But if you trust that he will learn even if he does make a mistake, and if you let him know that he can always come to you if he's not sure what to do, he may come to you as he grows. Or he may not. You can buy him a few books on relationships and leave them in his room without saying anything other than "I thought you might find some useful info in the books I left in your room."

Often, parents who feel the need to control their children are not passionately absorbed in their own life purpose. They worry so much because they do not have other positive and constructive things going on in their own lives. As a result, their children become their central focus, and healthy boundaries are not established. Older teenagers need to know that it is okay to be independent, and that their parents are always there for them if needed.

The critical answer to your question comes from two of your words: "my need." Replace the word "need" with the word "preference." Prefer to be a supportive parent who gives your older child roots and wings. Prefer to show your son that you are there for him by being around when he is home. Prefer to allow your son his personal independence because this is healthy. Obsessing over your child or anyone else does not help you or the other person. Replace that focus with something life-enhancing, something you enjoy, so that your life is more in balance. Then you will feel that need to control others gradually lessen as you live your life, make your own contributions, and set a positive example that your son can emulate. As you begin to feel more centered in self, that need to control will dissipate. You will be better able to handle watching your son go through his learning process with more trust, and he may come to you for guidance when he does not feel pressured or watched, knowing that you trust he will gain wisdom as he grows.

5. *Where do I find myself and not feel guilty for putting myself first?*

You can find yourself in only one place, and this is in your deepest heart. You can find yourself by listening to your real feelings about any matter or circumstance facing you. This is awakening to and discovering your truth. When you make it a habit to take time to notice how you feel, in the moment, you will find your true self. When you discover your true feelings and what you sense from others, you can follow what feels true and right for you in the moment, each moment that you are alive. This will strengthen you and build your sense of authentic self; then there will be no guilt in putting yourself first because it is only by listening to, honoring, and following your truth first— before the demands, responsibilities, or requests of others—that you will achieve inner peace.

Putting others before self is something I used to do when I was still a people pleaser; I put others first to feel validated by them and feel "good enough" by doing things that were asked of me even when I really didn't feel like doing them. I felt insecure, stressed, overloaded, and taxed. I was not living the truth of simply saying no when something was asked of me. I was afraid of not looking good. Once I learned to do only what I preferred to do based on what felt right for me, it became a lot easier to follow my truth and to put that truth first, ahead of the expectations I thought I had to fulfill in order to please others.

Sometimes we do have obligations, such as parenting or being there for a sick relative, obligations that might call for us to be there during a time of need. I feel this is important to honor, even if it might be over-loading or inconvenient at certain times. For example, you cannot tell your children that you don't feel like driving them to school or baseball practice; that would be child neglect. There is a difference between honor-ing your obligations and acceding to unnecessary requests from others.

The guilt comes from not feeling worthy as you are now, and wanting the approval of others. I certainly lived this way for many years until I learned that no one outside of me can validate me or cause me to feel more worthy. This is an inside job for me, for you, and for all other human beings.

In terms of putting yourself first, do only that which you feel inspired, excited, and passionate about. If you are not excited about it, do not do it. You do not owe people explanations. You can merely say that you are not available to do such-and-such.

That is all you need to say. Moreover, you are not responsible for the reactions other people have. Simply go within, notice how you really feel about the situa-tion, and follow that. Once you get into the habit of living this way, which is living your truth, the guilt that you have been feeling will begin to dissipate. Eventually, when you live and do only what feels true to you, the guilt will no longer exist.

6. *How can women know they are making wise choices when it comes to health care, hormones, and menopause? Where is the balance between old and*

New Age information? In my coaching practice, I find that so many women think they should avoid most forms of treatment, including bioidentical hormones, even though they are experiencing extreme symptoms (fatigue, lack of clarity, insomnia, depression, hot flashes, weight gain, emotional unbalance) that are significantly affecting their quality of life and well-being.

I believe that the old age and the New Age meet in bringing out the truth in the Information Age. A good way to inform women about health care would be to create an educational pamphlet or brochure describing particular symptoms and the alternative methods of treatment available. The brochure cannot be geared toward one form of treatment solely for monetary gain, but toward the best-known and most up-to-date methods available. Potential side effects of such treatments should also be described, so women can choose the best methods available.

7. *How do we heal ourselves as women? As nurturing creatures, we can get manipulated. As a survivor, I know that we neglect our own health and feelings in times of trauma. We wind up in trouble.*

Please know that no one can manipulate you without your consent. You have intuition and an inner knowing that transcends what your five senses or other people may be showing or telling you. In any circumstance, ask yourself how you feel. Sleep on a major decision, and ask the Divine for a new realization to come to you during sleep so you can have a clearer perspective when you wake up. Never allow yourself to be pressured into a decision. Never allow yourself to compromise on your truth and what feels right or wrong to you inside. Your inner truth cannot be negotiable. When people try to coerce or manipulate you, you can make a conscious choice to say no, to say that you do not feel comfortable with whatever is being asked of you.

As for your health, I am not a medical doctor, so I am not qualified to give you medical advice. But as a rule of thumb, listen to what your body is telling you! If you feel tired and drained, sleep. Get a full work-up by your medical doctor. You may be overdoing it on all levels; you may need to take inventory of your to-do list and eliminate what you truly do not want in your life anymore. I have witnessed many people who did not honor their real feelings, who ran themselves ragged, and then got physically ill.

It is your responsibility to pay attention to how you feel on all levels, intuitive, emotional, and physical. Once you start to pay attention to how you feel, and follow through by honoring your feelings in your actions, you will find that a lot of the manipulation will cease. You will no longer be trapped in a cycle of not honoring what your body, heart, and soul are telling you. This can greatly reduce your chances of attracting physical illness because you will be in tune with your self, following how you feel. You will greatly enhance your life on all levels.

8. *How do I let go of worrying way too much about what people think about me, the way I live my life, what I say, how I look, and all?*

This is actually a lot simpler than you may realize. First, what other people think comes solely and completely from their own perceptions, and there are as many different perceptions as there are people. How could you possibly please everyone? You cannot. For example, suppose you change the color of your hair and ask ten people to tell you what they think of the new color. Five may love it. Three may think your hair looked better before. And two may think it should be an entirely different color. Would you change your hair color to match the personal preferences of the other people? If you did, you would drive yourself crazy, not to mention causing a lot of wear and tear on your hair!

You are the one who has to be pleased, not the other people. You have to live your life the way it suits you, and you alone. If other people do not like it (so long as you are causing no harm to others, which I am sure you are not), then they will have to deal with their own feelings. You are not responsible for how other people think and feel about the way you live, worship, speak, or behave.

Many years ago I used to twist myself into whatever form would please others. When I met a man who liked brunettes, I changed my naturally blonde hair color to dark brown. Then I felt as if that wasn't the real me, and the change didn't cause him to show interest in me anyway, so I went back to blonde. When I met a man who loved country music, I went to a music store and bought about ten country music cassettes (CDs hadn't been invented yet). That relationship didn't last more than three months. The only reason I am sharing this with you is to show you that I finally learned my lesson. I learned that I had to listen to the music *I* liked. I had to find the courage to stick with being an author when relatives told me to "get a real job." I had to find my truth, and so do you. Once I began to pay attention to my truth and follow it, my self-esteem started to skyrocket. I stopped worrying about pleasing other people to gain their acceptance and approval; instead, I began to live my truth and share authentically. Can I please everyone? Of course not. When we learn that we are all in this life to be and express our genuine selves, that life is about the joy we feel as a result of our being and expressing, we stop worrying so much about what other people think because it is completely beyond our control. Moreover, once you become your own best friend, by living and following what feels true and right to you, you will start to feel a lot more confident and a lot less concerned about the reactions of others.

The life purpose of some people is to rock the boat. People like Nelson Mandela, who was imprisoned for speaking out to end apartheid. Following his truth to see all people treated equally regardless of their skin color was more important to him than the popular opinion of those who ruled his country at the time.

My personal rule of thumb is to not concern myself with what other people think of me. My only concern is that my motives are pure and that I am making a difference from my heart.

As long as you live purely from the heart and follow your truth on all levels of your life, your self-confidence will continue to strengthen. You will eventually reach the point of accepting that people have their own perspectives, they are entitled to those perspectives, and it is not your responsibility to try to control them. Your only responsibility is to live your truth. This will keep you rock solid in your self-confidence and self-worth for the rest of your life.

9. *I do feel I know myself after sixty-five years, although I can lose touch with myself when I'm tired or stressed. But situations come up when I feel compelled to explain myself, and when I do, I feel weakened, as if having to explain takes away from "just being." How do we project enough radiant confidence to keep others from either misunderstanding us or asking us to explain ourselves? For example, I am easily overly stimulated. I know I have this trait and must set my limits. People misunderstand or become offended when I have to leave or go off by myself for a while. I hate to explain why I need to do this.*

The most crucial thing for you to know and always remember is that you do not have to explain yourself to anyone, at any time. All you need to do is state your truth: "I'm going to get some rest now; I'll touch base with you in the next few days." You are not responsible for the feelings and reactions of others; therefore, you do not need to explain yourself. You cannot prevent others from misunderstanding you or asking you to explain yourself. This is completely beyond your control. It seems that you want others to understand you, but what you must realize is that the only person who needs to understand you is you. Whether others do or do not understand is beyond your control. Simply do as you wish, without an explanation. You are not under an obligation to explain yourself to anyone, ever. Your only obligation is to do as you prefer, when you prefer. You do not prefer to explain yourself to others; therefore, explanations are not necessary.

10. *When you have gotten to the point of feeling healthy and whole from the inside out and really know what you deserve, how do you handle and communicate with people who do not fall into this new category? Do you cut them out of your life? What if you can't because they are your ex and you have children? Is this just one more lesson we are to learn after we have grown into our own truths?*

Certain people whom you have outgrown will naturally flow out of your life as you attract new friends with whom you have more in common. With other people, such as relatives or an ex with whom you share children, all you need to do is have cordial communication when necessary. When you grow in a new direction or outgrow other people, you will gradually have less and less contact with them. Some of your high school friends are clearly not in your life right now. You moved in different directions. It is the same when you outgrow certain friends. Your interests may have changed, and so you may not care to engage in the same kinds of conversations and activities as before.

If someone calls you, please do be kind and cordial to them. If they want to get together, you can simply say that you are busy with other things or that you are really not interested in doing whatever activity they suggest. You can say, "I lost interest in that." This lets people know how you feel. Because you no longer share the same interests, the contact will fade.

As you grow and evolve, do not judge others. People grow at different rates; some stay stuck for decades. But all people are doing the best they can with the level of personal and spiritual growth they have at any time. The best way to view such people is with loving compassion. Wish them the best from your heart, as you gracefully carry on with your own life according to your own truth.

Chapter 10

Knowing Your Nature

K nowing yourself requires one act only: self-truth at all times.

You are always divinely guided whether or not you believe in anything of a divine nature. You are guided through your intuition, your gut instincts and feelings, and your inner perceptions, all of which carry far more wisdom than anything that exists outside of you in the sea of life's constant changes.

It is imperative that you know your true nature if you are ever to know yourself.

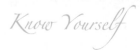

Your nature is unlimited. It is Source energy. It is bound by nothing more than your beliefs, thoughts, and perceived limitations. Therefore, it is never bound; it is boundless and eternal.

The wellspring of divine nature that exists within your soul is your true nature, and you are All That Is in physical form.

Do not believe that you are limited. Like Moses who parted the Red Sea and Jesus who healed the blind, you too are of divine essence. As a divine being of eternal spirit, it is your birthright to know that there is no circumstance before you that you cannot overcome. Moreover, many of the experiences before you are there precisely to show you that you can overcome anything, so long as you believe in your unlimited power, which is the truth of your being.

Truth and Spirit do not play favorites. The sun sets over the heads of those who know their true nature as it does over those who have yet to discover their indwelling divinity sans ritual. You are asked to bow to nothing but your indwelling spirit of truth. When you come to know and believe that your birthright is the same as that of any person you may favor, you will come to know that you, too, have that same essence in your spirit, in your soul, and especially in your mind. Your mind is forever connected to divine ideas and a wellspring of inspiration. You have only to ask and then listen to the answer that comes into your mind.

It is one thing to *look* whole, radiant, and supremely confident and another to *be* in the wisdom of your wholeness, confident in your unlimited abilities, and radiant in your expression of those abilities that bring you the most joy as you serve from your heart.

Service is not servitude. Service is being in alignment with your truth and expressing your truth according to what brings the most joy to your heart. When you know that you are making a difference, even by the simple act of smiling, you will also know that the spirit which exists as part of every breath you take is unlimited in its expression in every area of your life.

As a woman, you have the ability to combine all of your natural talents, strengths, abilities, and attributes as you express your wholeness. You are to obey no one except the One in your heart, which is your divine truth.

You cannot mock yourself and expect to simultaneously express your grandest essence. You cannot indulge in negative mind banter and expect to have wisdom flow from your lips. You cannot be a radiant example of divine essence when you mock and judge the person in the mirror.

To know yourself requires an earnest desire to rise above old societal conditioning and into your eternal truth, truth that will be a beacon for others whom you hope will free themselves from the shackles of disbelief in self.

Now it is your turn to think straight. To turn your mind to thoughts of creative solutions, to turn your mind inward toward your soul, and ask the One with-

in for guidance. You can call it The One God, Spirit, All That Is; but the one name that encompasses all of these is I AM. Your name IS the One indwelling spirit from which all inspiration emanates. You are the physical embodiment of Source, Divine Spirit, God, All That Is.

If you view yourself as anything less than divine, you are viewing yourself through muddied glasses. You are supreme, and so is every other human being. You are more than your circumstances. And you are the sole creator of your circumstances. Begin to view yourself as a divine co-creator, and you will come to know the truth of your being. Begin to view yourself as the One who can turn around any seeming negativity and create a positive outcome that both you and those around you can celebrate as the triumph of the spiritual and human spirit.

You are the spirit, and Spirit is always within you. Think of inspiration rather than desperation. Think of your boundless imagination and how, one step at a time, one moment at a time, you can begin to rise like a phoenix from yesterday's despair.

Remember at all times that you came into this life to be and express every divine idea, and set no limits on your divine expression. See yourself as the answer, because the answer is within you, housed within your heart and soul. It is, however, your mind that carries out the instructions to your being. So your mind must have a single focus. Your mind must focus on the here and now while looking in the direction you are headed. You cannot travel north and south simultaneously.

It is the same in your life. You cannot rise and sink at the same time. The thoughts you choose to run through your mind are what determine the direction of your life. No one has any power over you so long as you stand in your truth and claim your birthright to your own divine essence.

Remember at all times that you are divine. Remember at all times that jewels of wisdom are to be gleaned from mistakes. Remember that no matter what you see before you, it is completely within your power to choose the direction in which you would like to travel, and it is your birthright to enjoy every single moment of your journey.

But the goal alone is not what matters. What matters is the joy in expressing all of who you are while on your journey. This might seem to be a statement that you have heard before; but now, view yourself as a boundless, eternal expression of the divine, and you will come to know the truth about yourself. Take all limits out of your thought system and replace them with the joys you wish to experience. Have the courage to walk, talk, stand, sit, and play however you want to, so long as you bring no harm to others or to yourself. Remember that if anyone tries to harm you in any fashion, it is your responsibility to walk away as fast as you can, so that you can tend to what matters most in your heart, rather than wasting your precious hours trying to get back at others. You are too valuable to waste your time in negative fights. If you are fighting for justice, *be* justice, and speak of justice. Your example will have a ripple effect; your truth will resonate

with all who hear it, and they will understand your words.

Know with absolute certainty that as you come to know your essence and your joys, you will have more courage to express them in all areas of your life.

One thing you must always remember: there is an indwelling divine spirit within you that no condition can ever extinguish. Find the divine within your heart, and declare to yourself that you are a divine being. It is then and only then that you will express on the outside all you are within. It is then and only then that you will be remembered for standing in your own light, and you will be remembered as a beacon for others, even if they may never have known you personally. Your spirit is eternal. Your words do have a ripple effect. Your actions count. You count. Remember how sacred you are. The divine spirit in your heart is your life force. If the divine is your life force, then you are the divine. Now, it is time to play, and to celebrate every joy you wish to experience. Celebrate your divinity with joy. Your smile and radiance will touch those around you, and you will finally come to know that you are not only an expression of the divine, you are the divine giving expression.

Notes and Personal Realizations

Notes and Personal Realizations

Notes and Personal Realizations

_____

_____

_____

_____

_____

_____

_____

_____

_____

_____

_____

_____

_____

_____

Notes and Personal Realizations

Notes and Personal Realizations

_____

_____

_____

_____

_____

_____

_____

_____

_____

_____

_____

_____

_____

_____

Notes and Personal Realizations

Notes and Personal Realizations

_____

_____

_____

_____

_____

_____

_____

_____

_____

_____

_____

_____

_____

Notes and Personal Realizations

_____

_____

_____

_____

_____

_____

_____

_____

_____

_____

_____

_____

_____

Notes and Personal Realizations

Notes and Personal Realizations

Notes and Personal Realizations

Notes and Personal Realizations

About the Author

Barbara Rose, Ph.D. most widely known as "Born To Inspire," is a best selling author and internationally recognized expert in the field of personal transformation, relationships and spiritual/ human potential. A pioneering force in incorporating Higher Self Communication the study and integration of humanity's God-Nature into modern personal growth and spiritual evolution.

Her highly acclaimed books, public speaking events, tele-seminars, widely published articles, and intensives have transformed the lives of thousands across the globe. Barbara is known for providing life-changing answers, quick practical coaching and deep spiritual wisdom to people worldwide. She is the founder of IHSC – Institute of Higher Self Communication, *inspire!* Magazine, Rose Humanitarian Alliance, and The Rose Group publishing company.

Barbara holds a Ph.D. in Metaphysics and works in cooperation with some of the greatest spiritual leaders of our time, to uplift the spiritual consciousness of humanity. Visit her Web site at *www.borntoinspire.com.*